AF478939

Well, stop still, people, and listen to me:

I wanna tell you 'bout a tragedy,

November twenty-second, sixty-three,

In a day that will always stay with me.

On Friday at noon in Dallas town,

A bullet struck, then struck him down,

Oh, with the president, when he lost his life,

Eh, by his side was Jackie, his wife.

That Awful Day in Dallas
BROTHER THERMON RUTH AND THE HARMONEERS

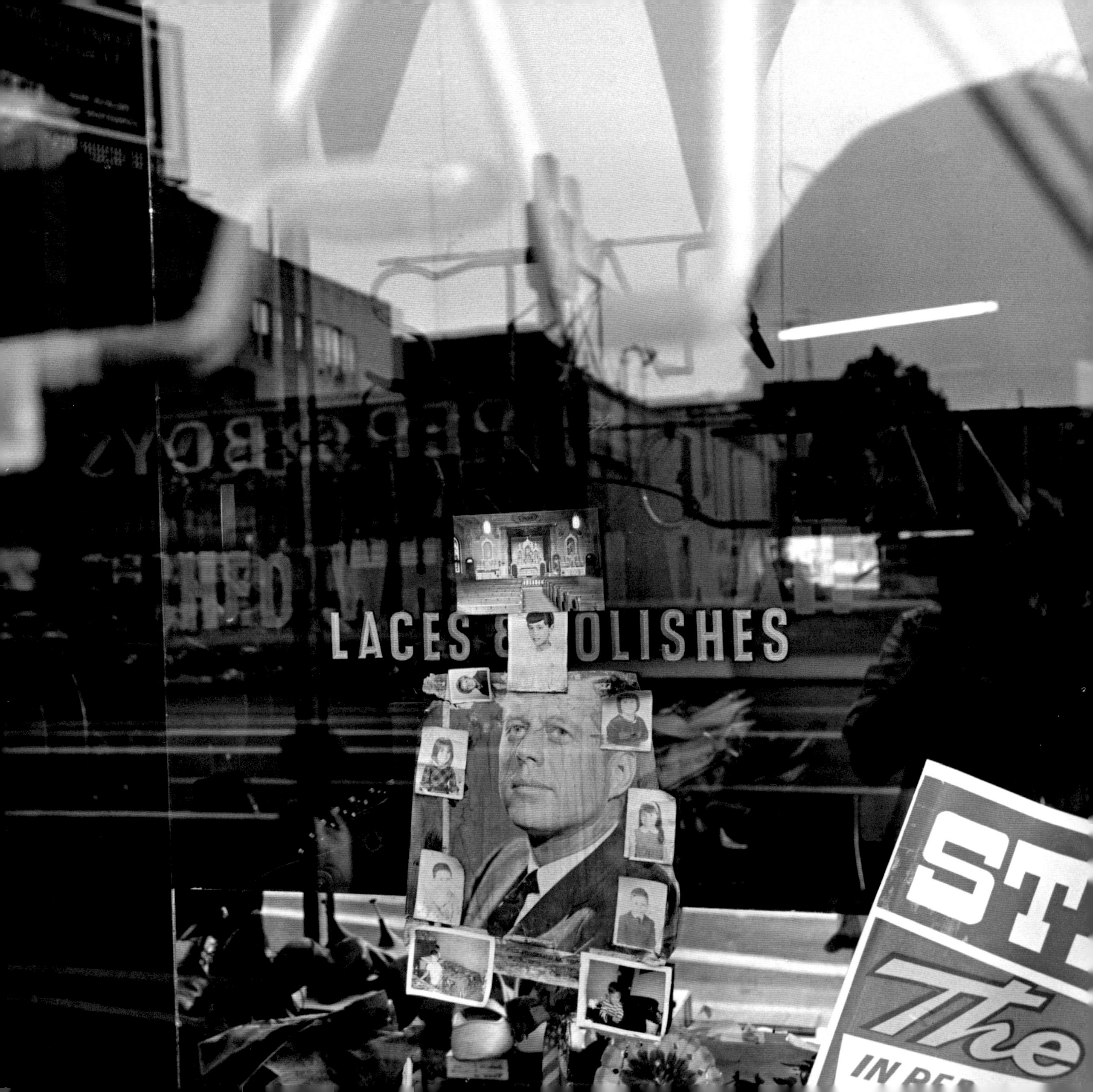
LACES & OLISHES
ST
The

jfk a photographic memoir

LEE FRIEDLANDER

YALE UNIVERSITY ART GALLERY
NEW HAVEN

DISTRIBUTED BY
YALE UNIVERSITY PRESS
NEW HAVEN AND LONDON

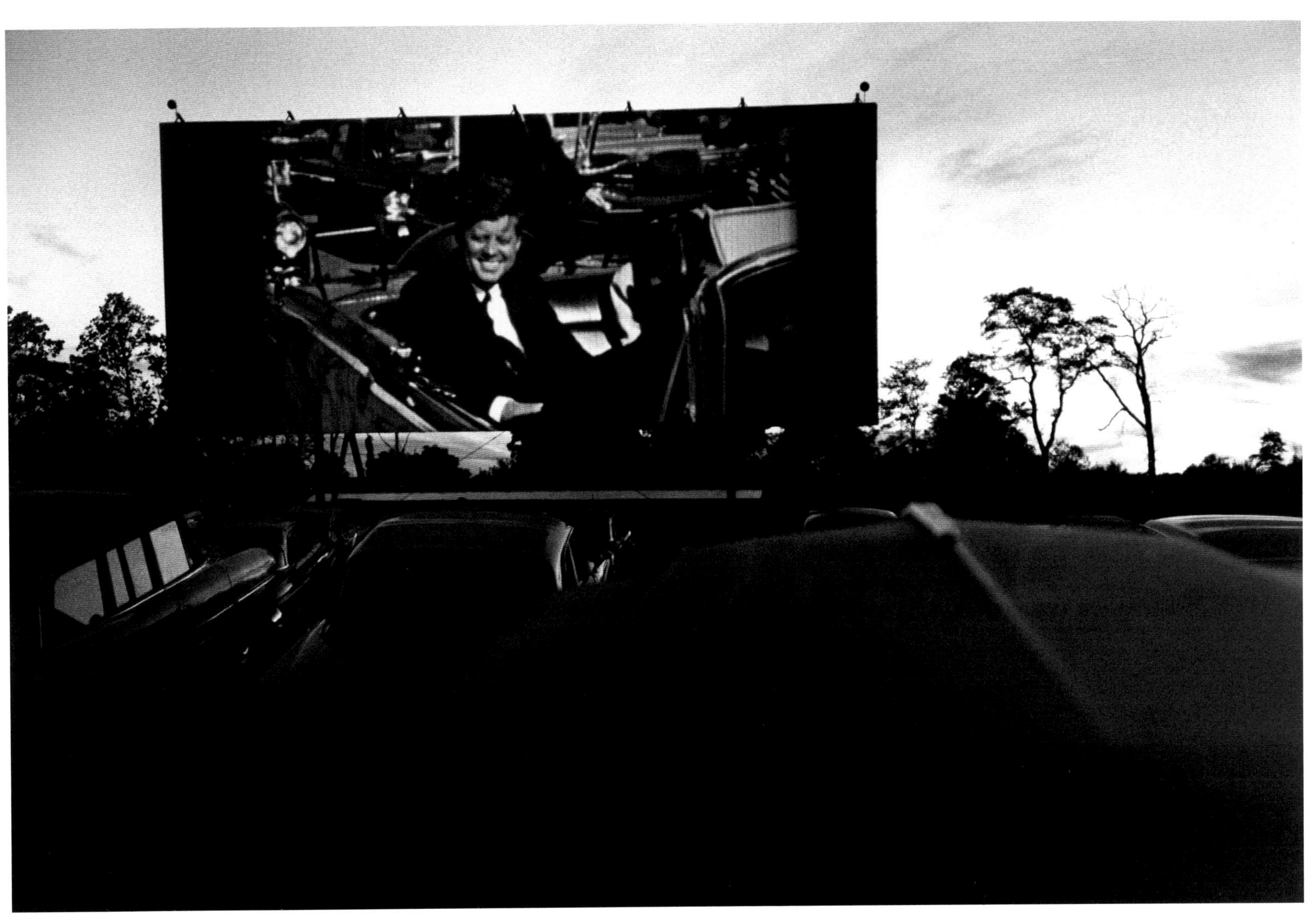

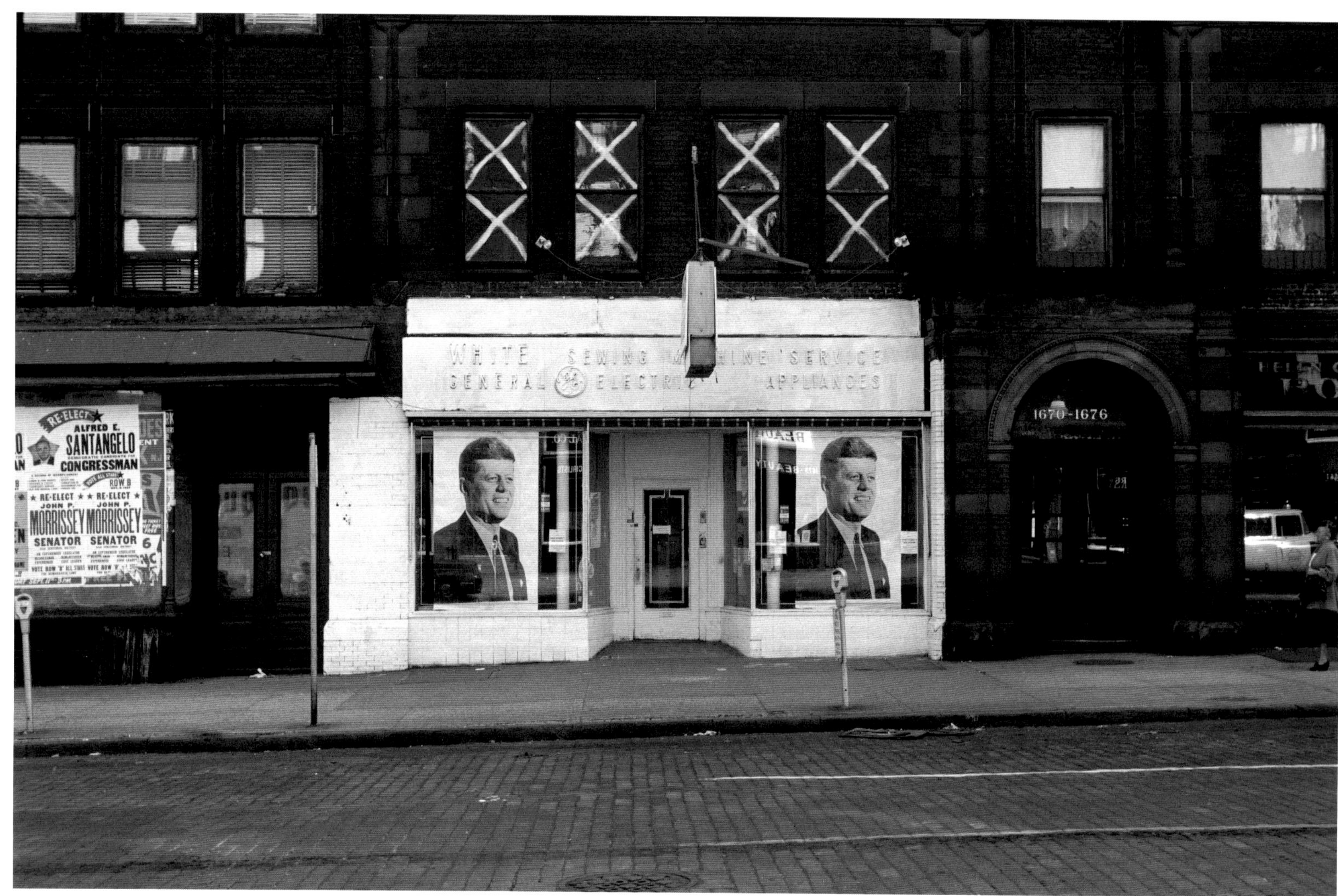

WHITE SEWING MACHINE SERVICE
GENERAL ELECTRIC APPLIANCES
1670-1676
RE-ELECT ★
ALFRED E.
SANTANGELO
DEMOCRATIC CANDIDATE FOR
CONGRESSMAN
ROW B
★ RE-ELECT ★ ★ RE-ELECT ★
JOHN P. JOHN P.
MORRISSEY MORRISSEY
SENATOR SENATOR
VOTE ROW "B" ALL STARS VOTE ROW B
6

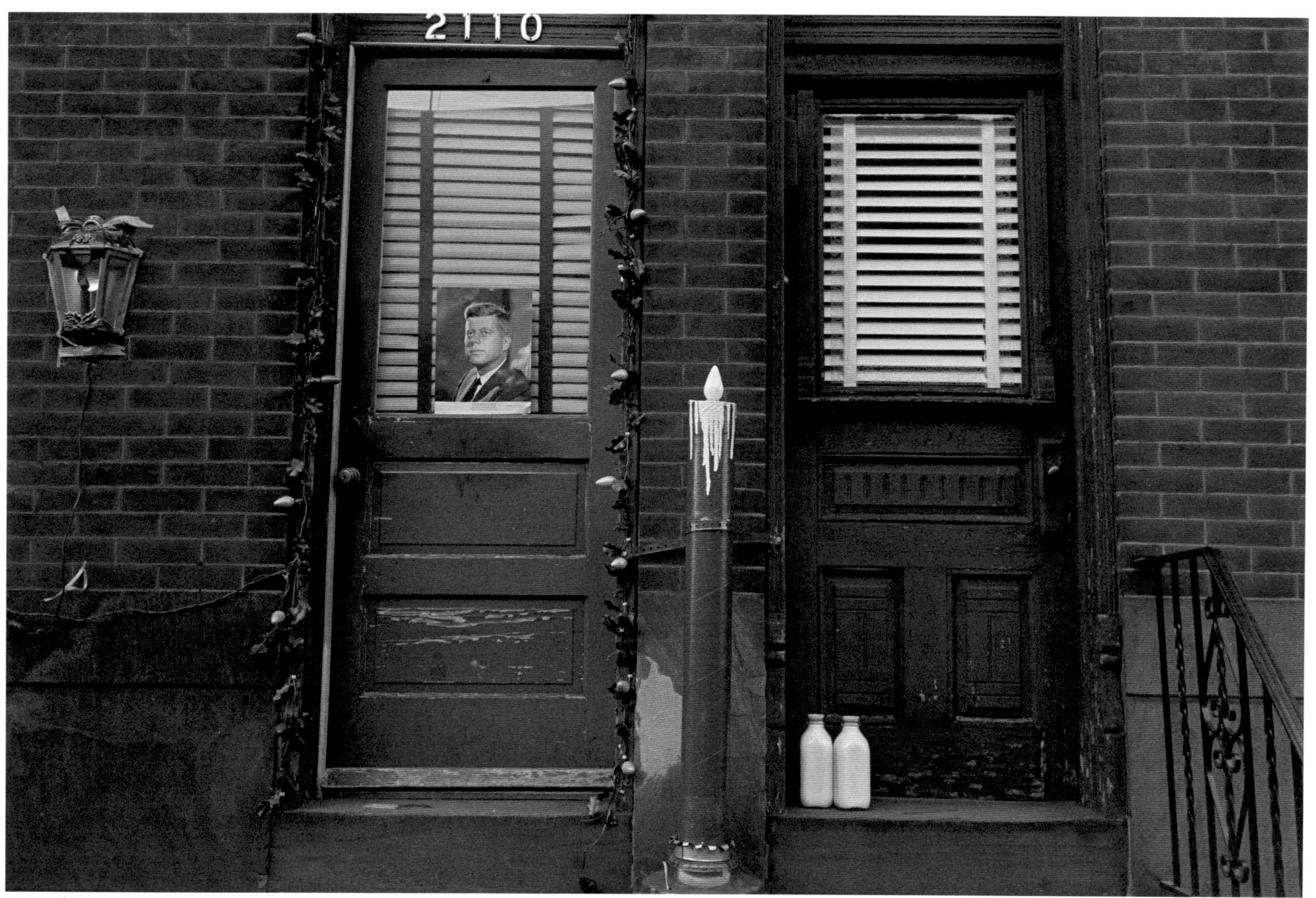

2110

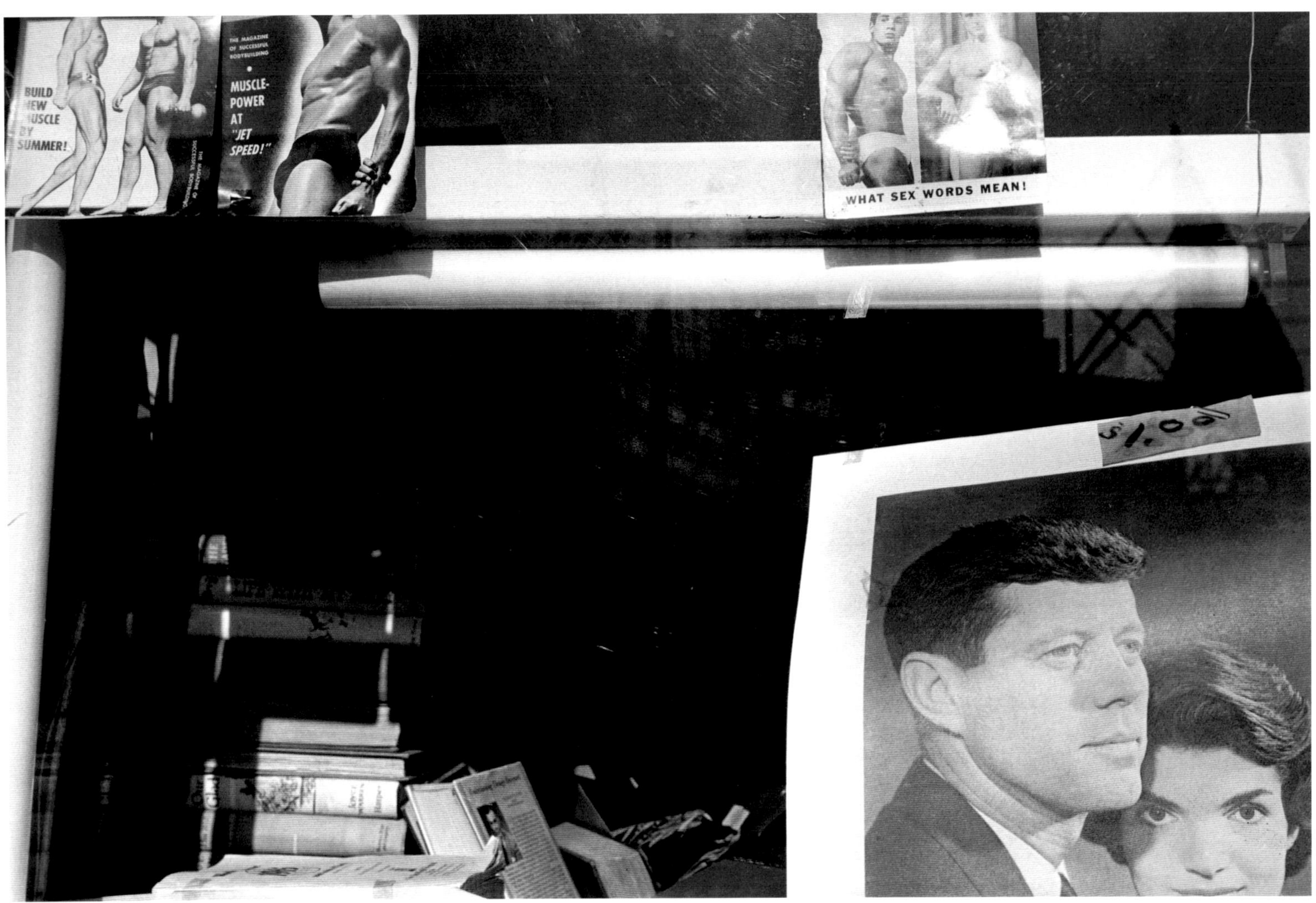
BUILD
NEW
MUSCLE
BY
SUMMER!
THE MAGAZINE OF SUCCESSFUL BODYBUILDING
MUSCLE-
POWER
AT
"JET
SPEED!"
WHAT SEX WORDS MEAN!
$1.00

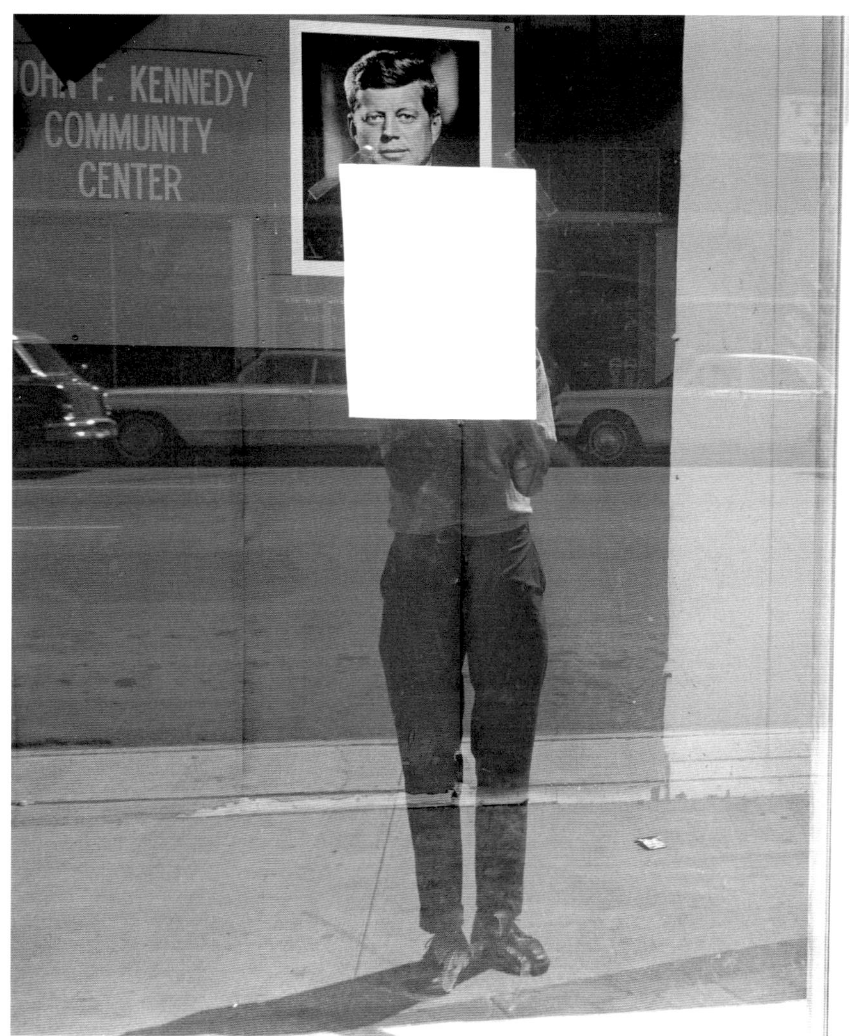

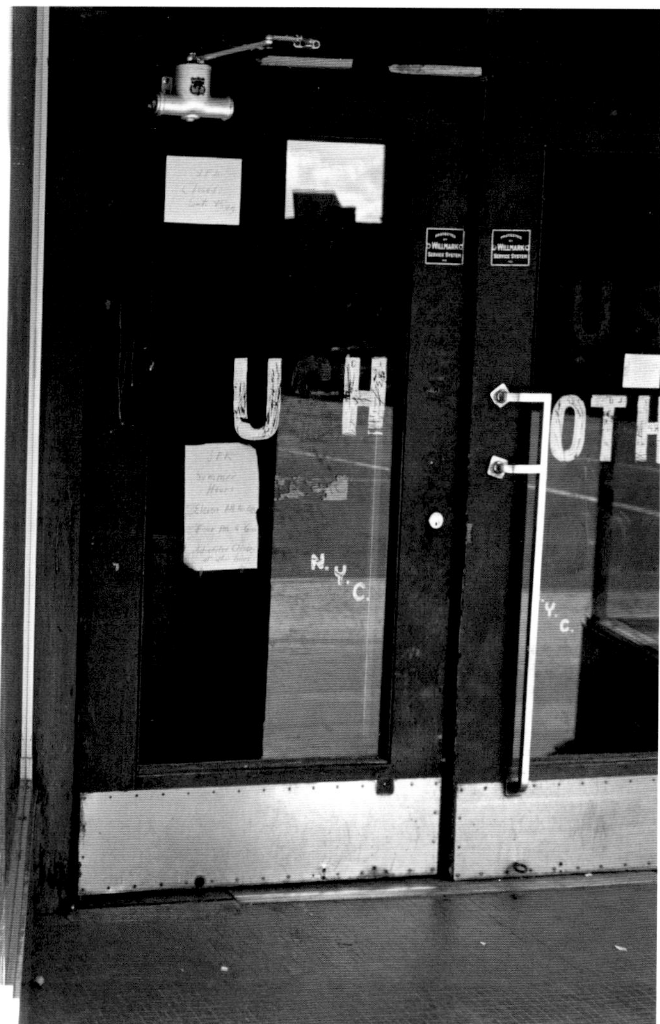

N.Y.C.
N.Y.C.

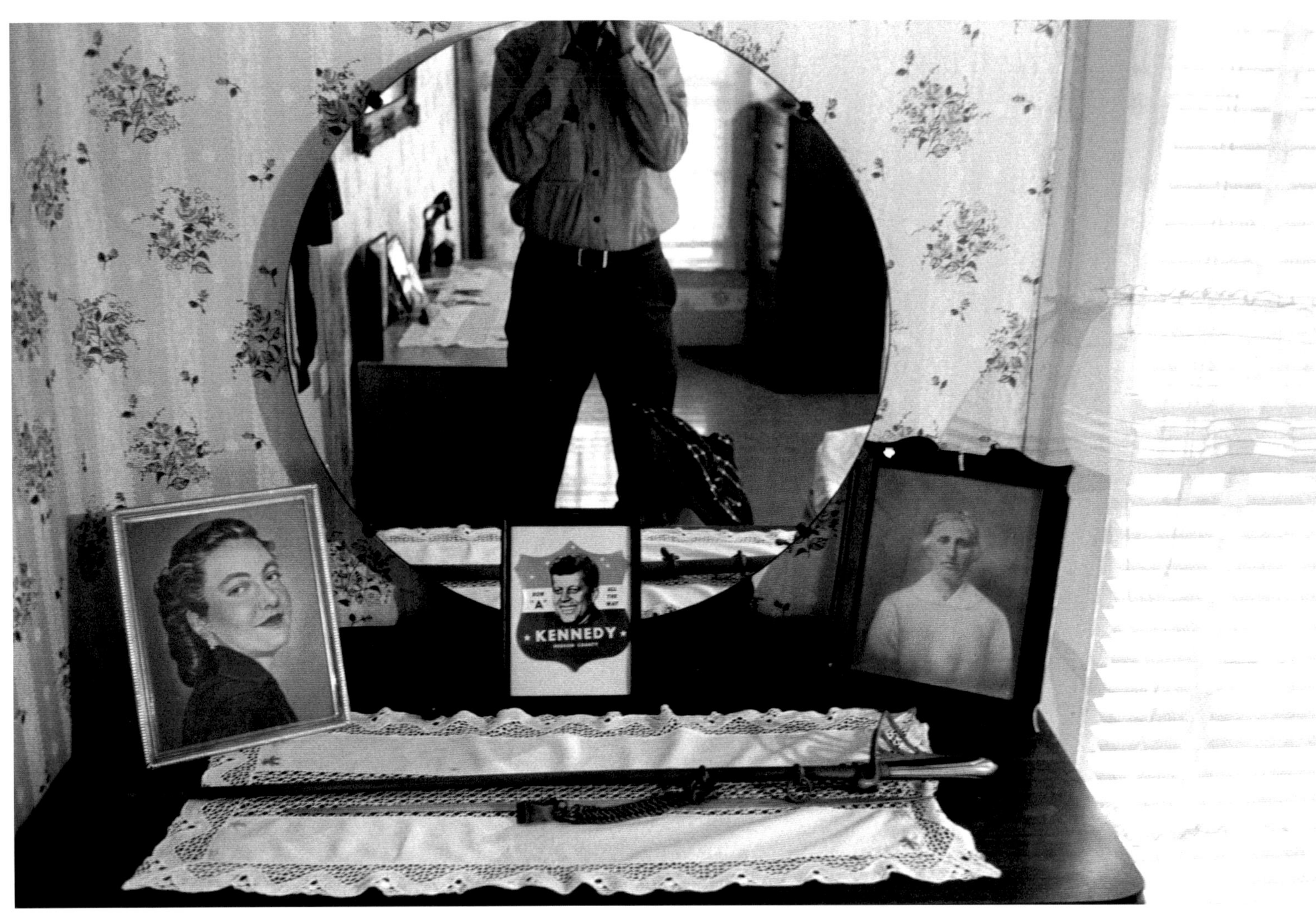

NOW
A
ALL THE WAY
KENNEDY
MARION COUNTY

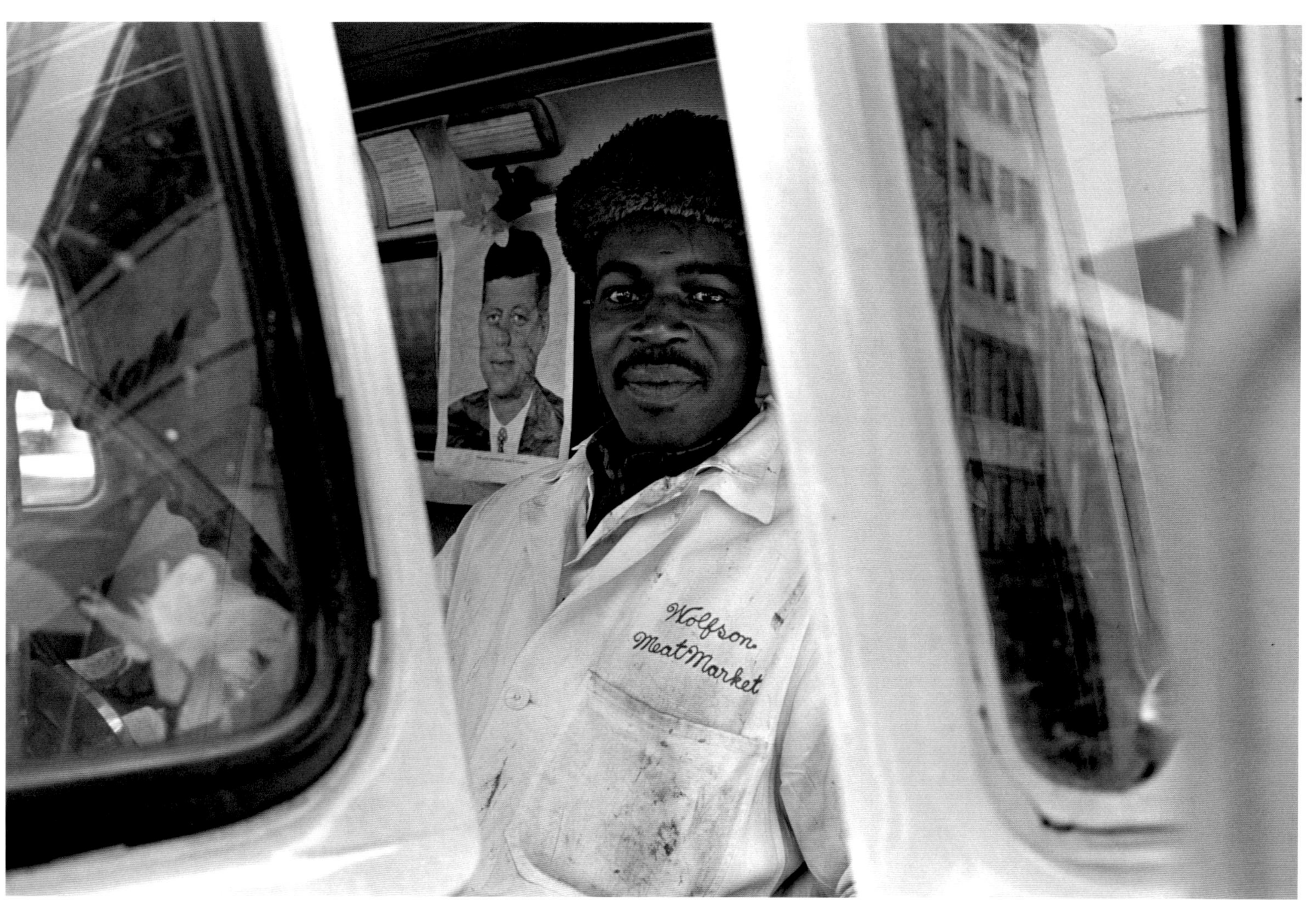

Wolfson
Meat Market

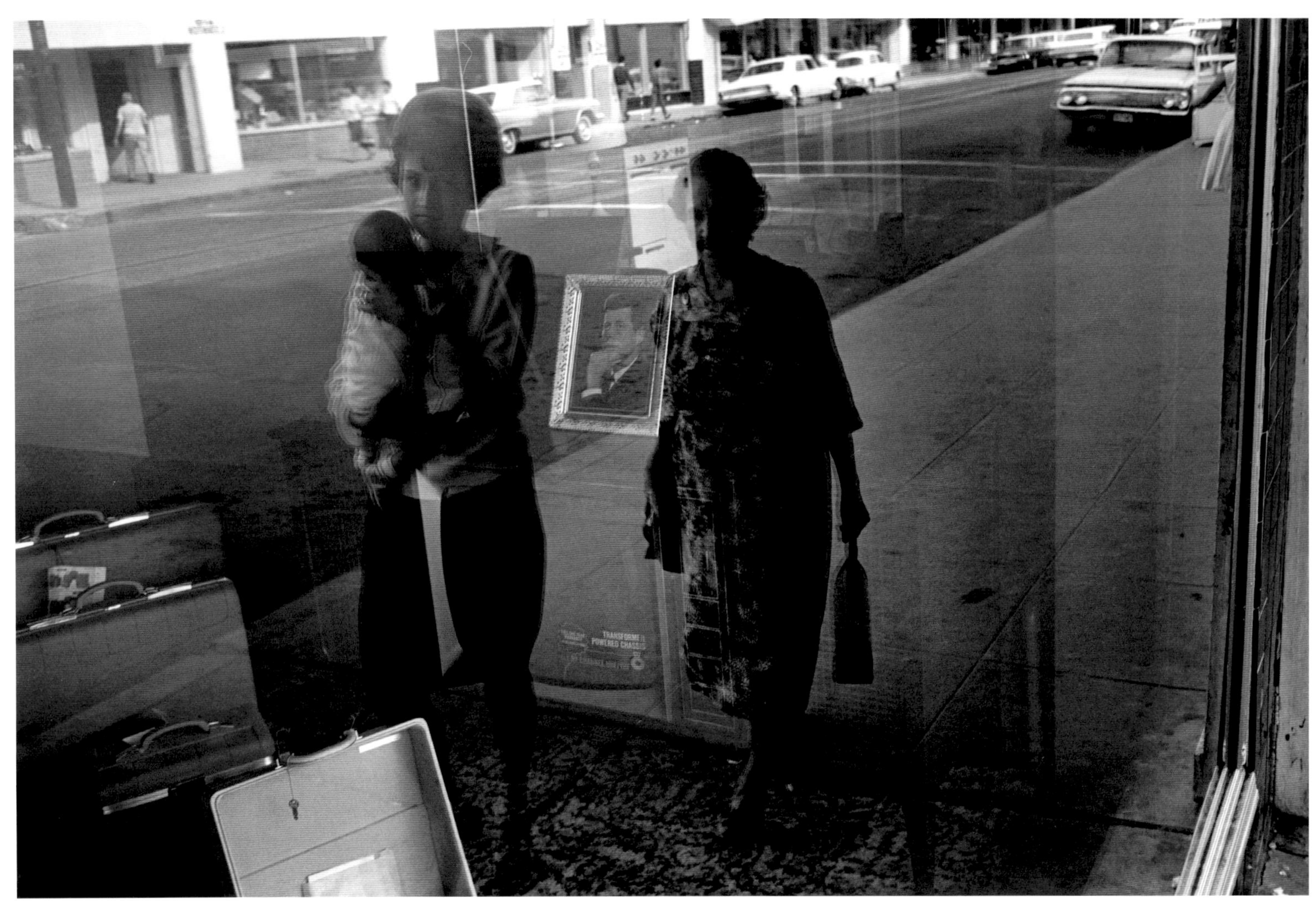

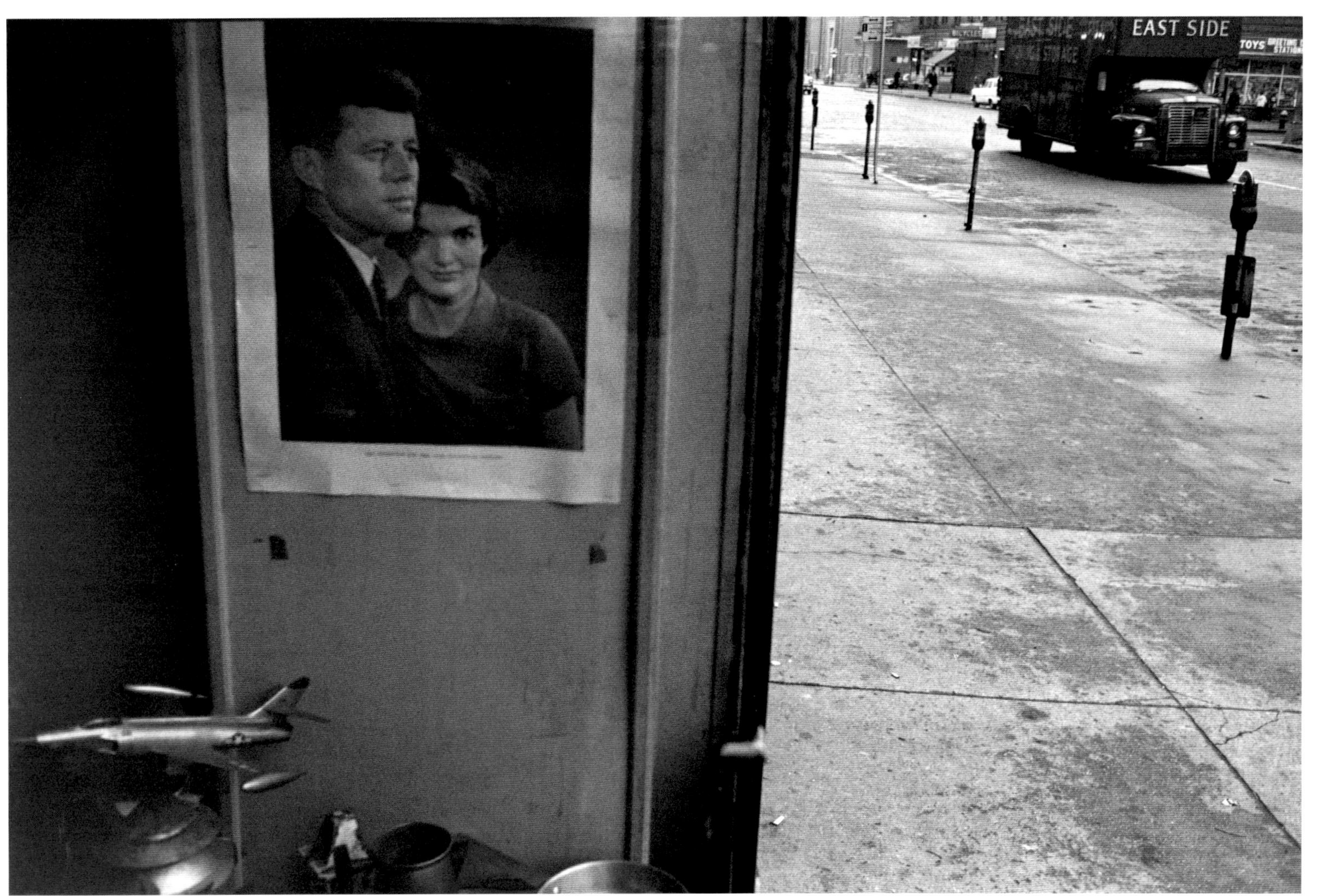

EAST SIDE
TOYS

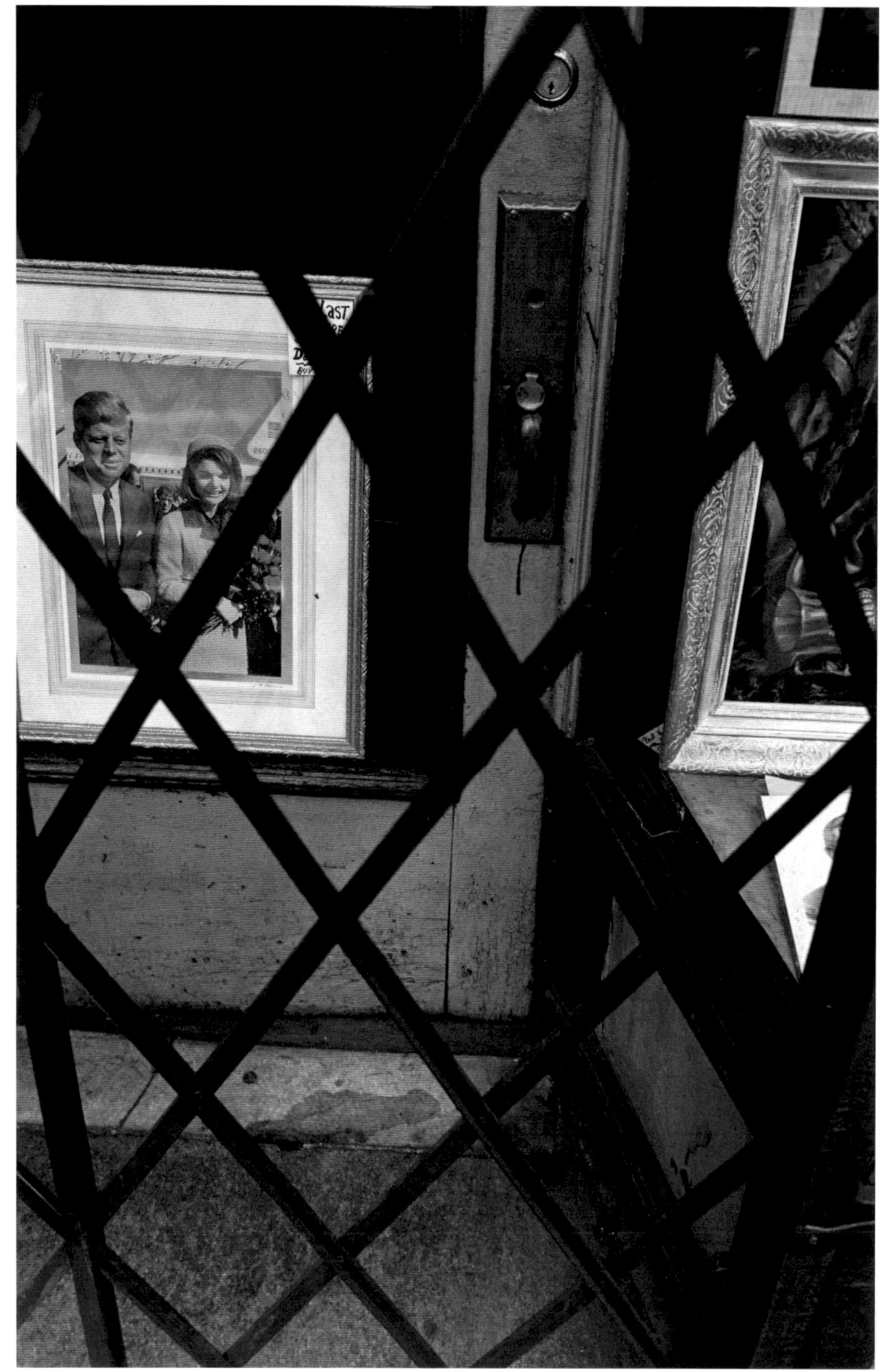

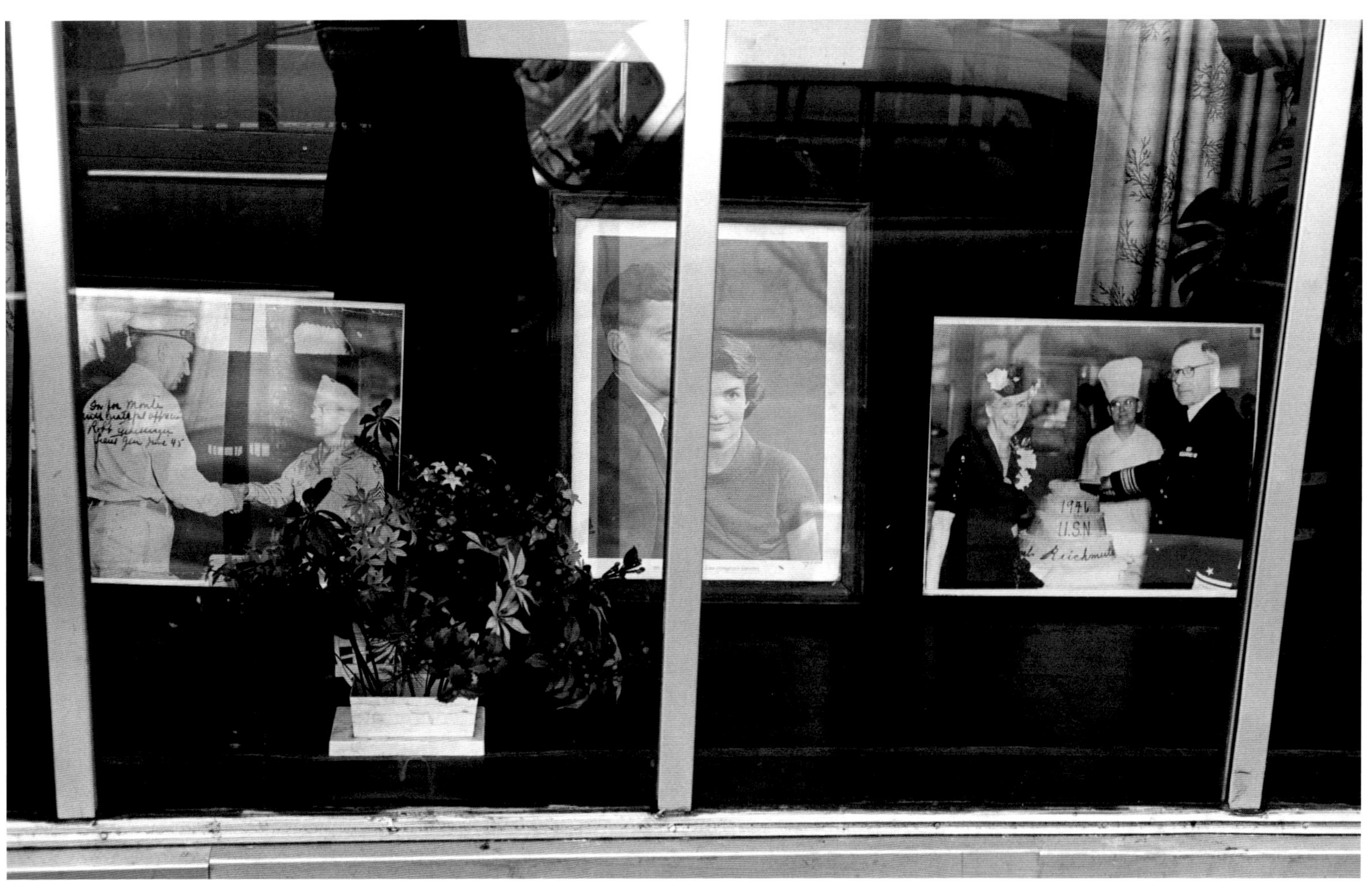

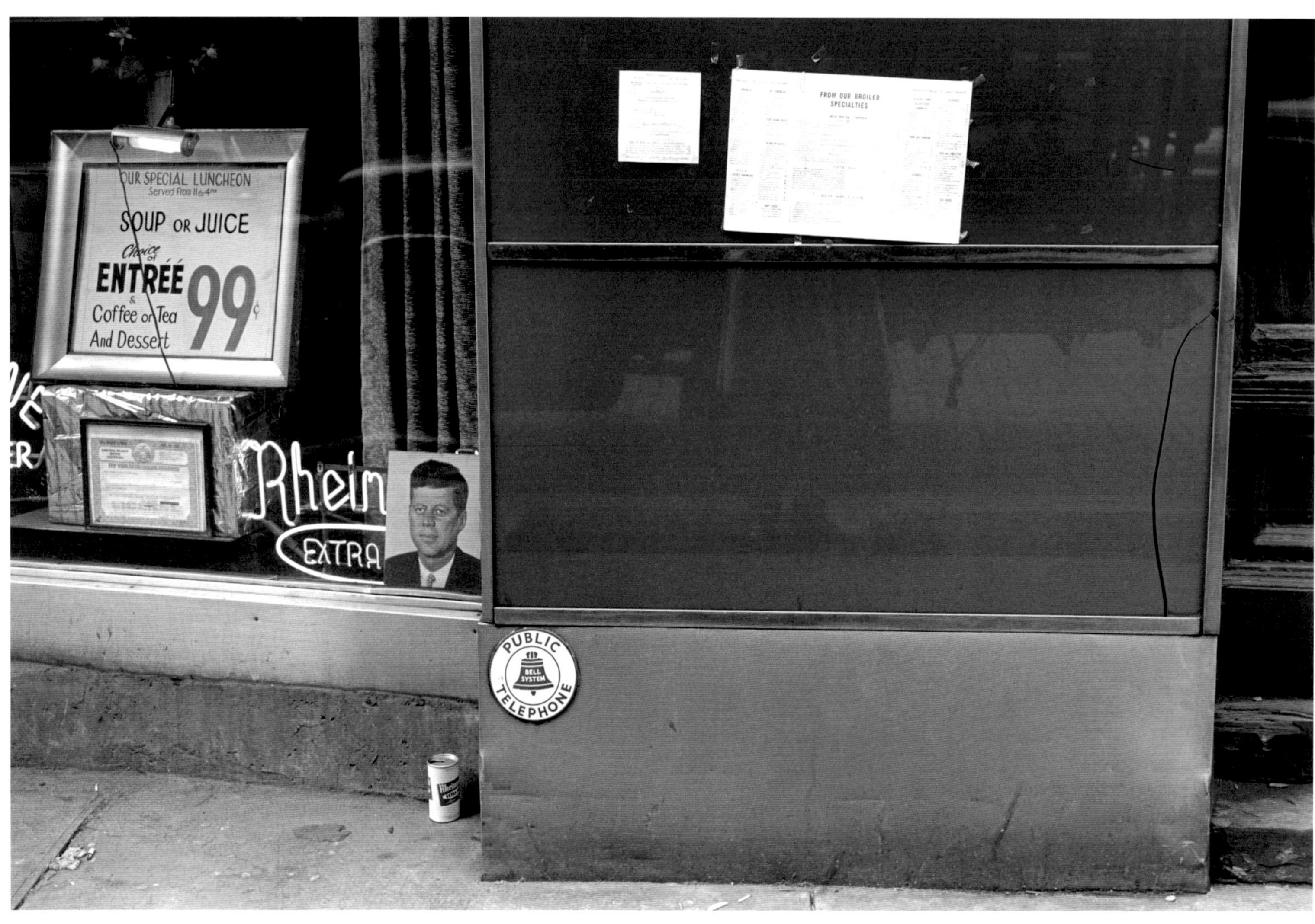
OUR SPECIAL LUNCHEON
Served From 11 to 4
SOUP OR JUICE
Choice of
ENTRÉE
&
Coffee or Tea
And Dessert
99¢
Rhein
EXTRA
PUBLIC
BELL SYSTEM
TELEPHONE
FROM OUR BROILED
SPECIALTIES

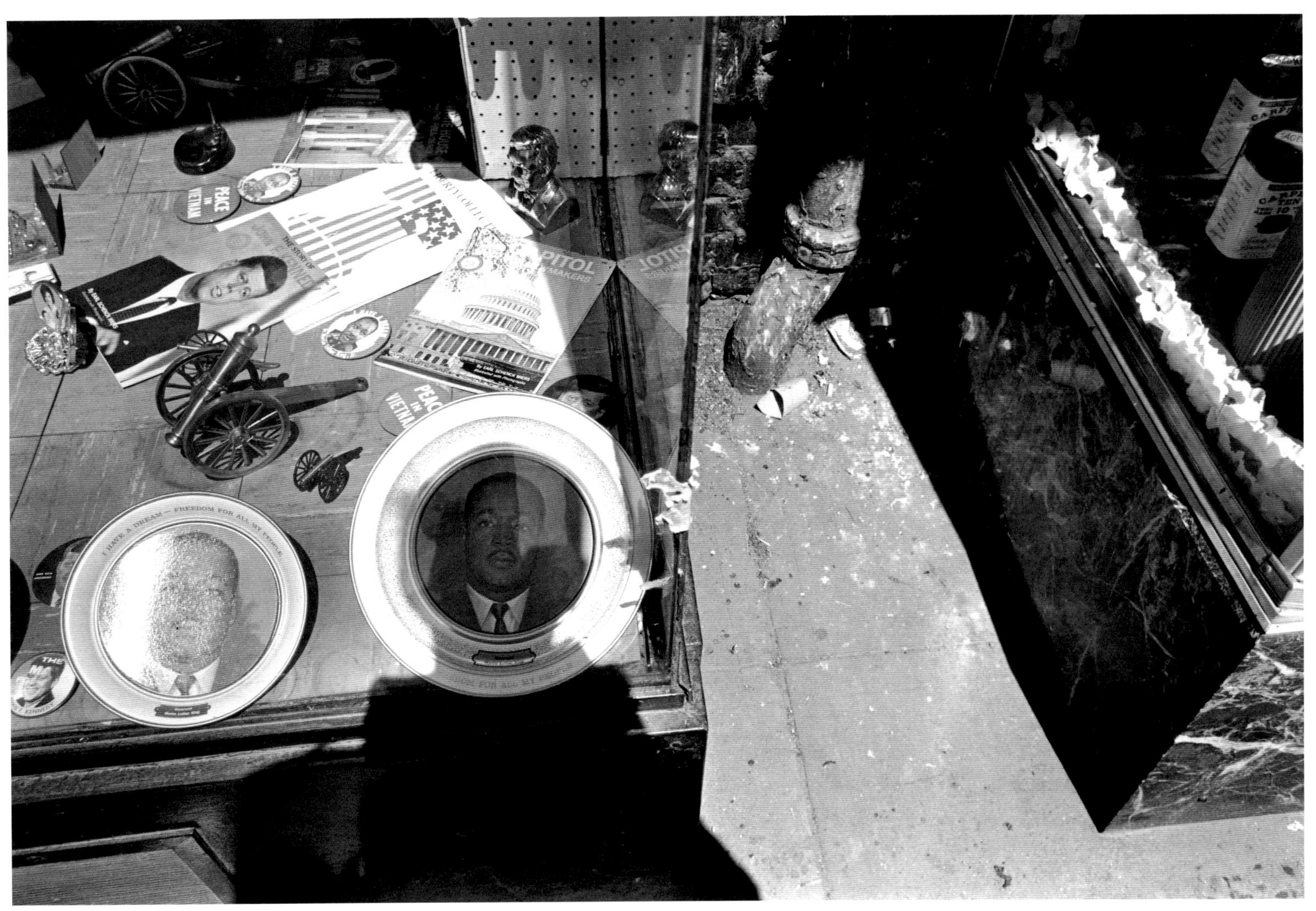

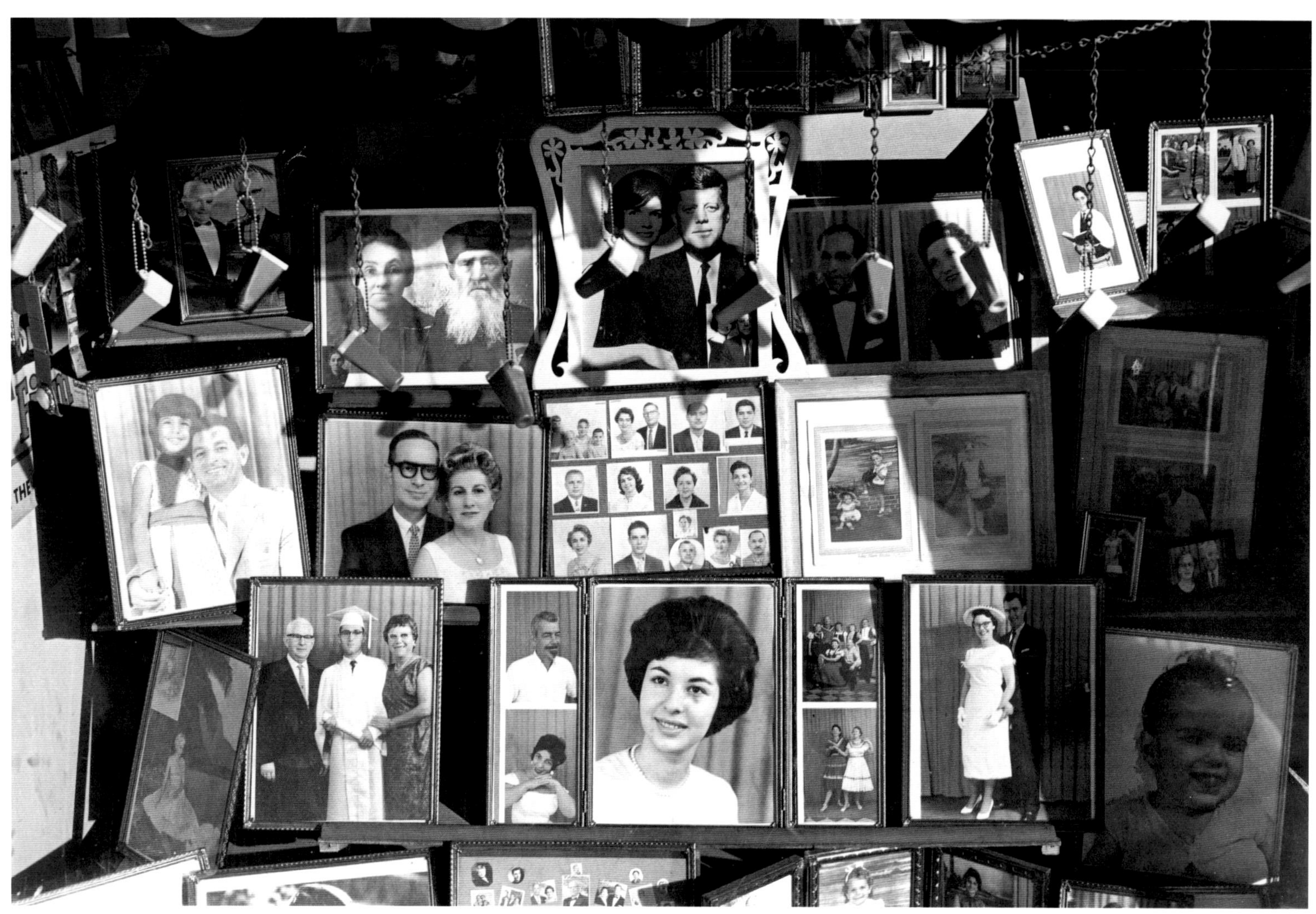

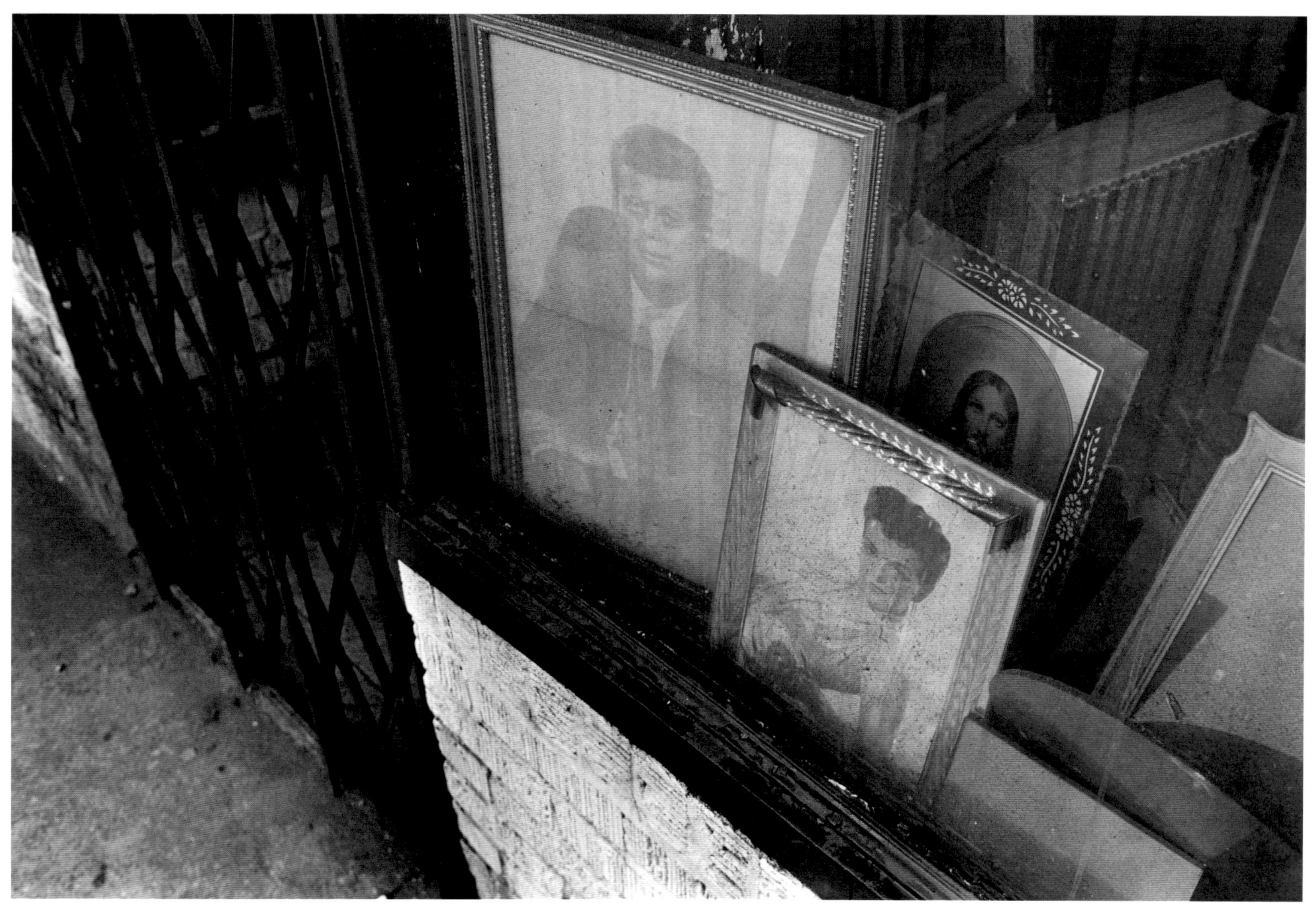

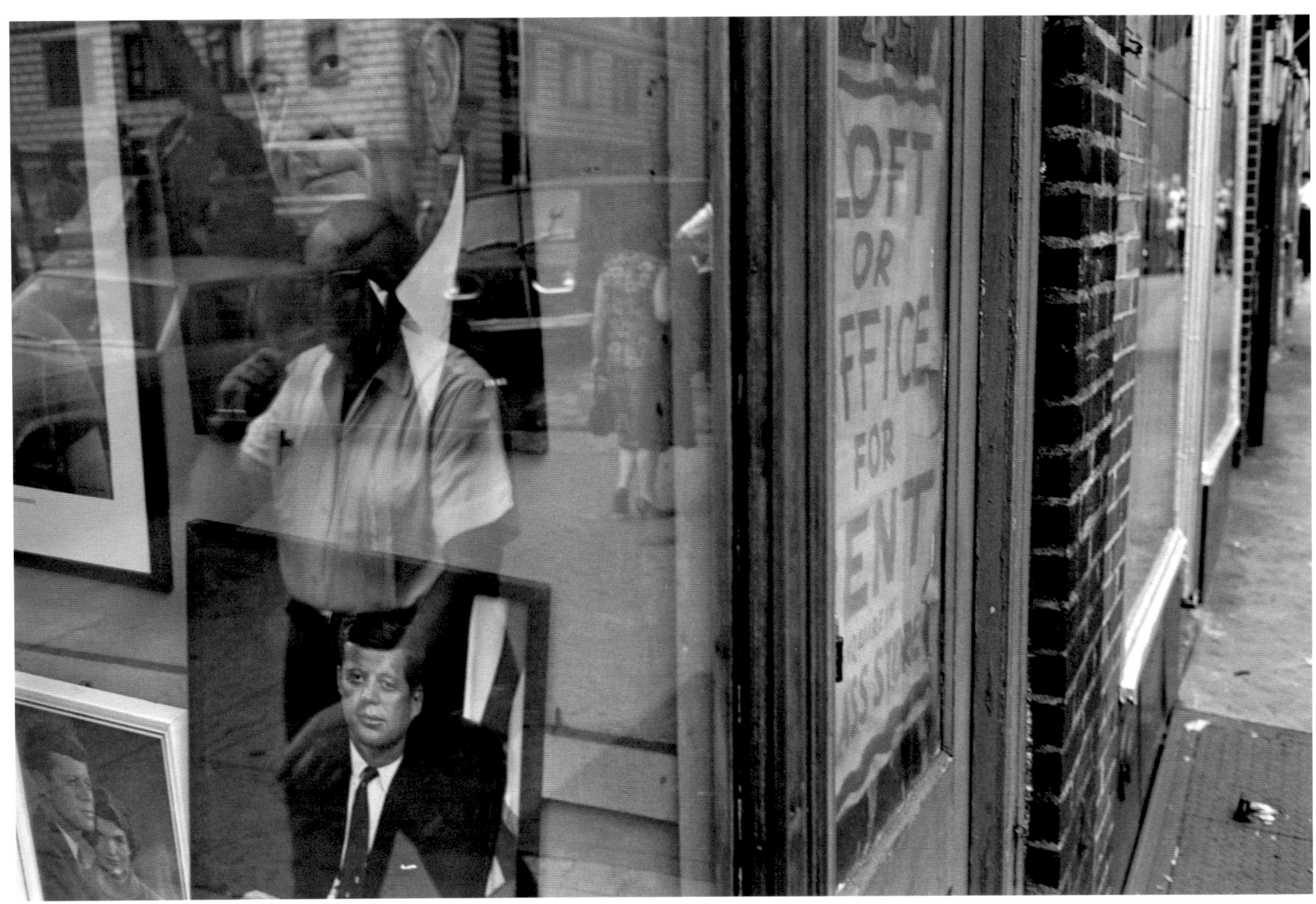

LOFT
OR
FFICE
FOR
ENT

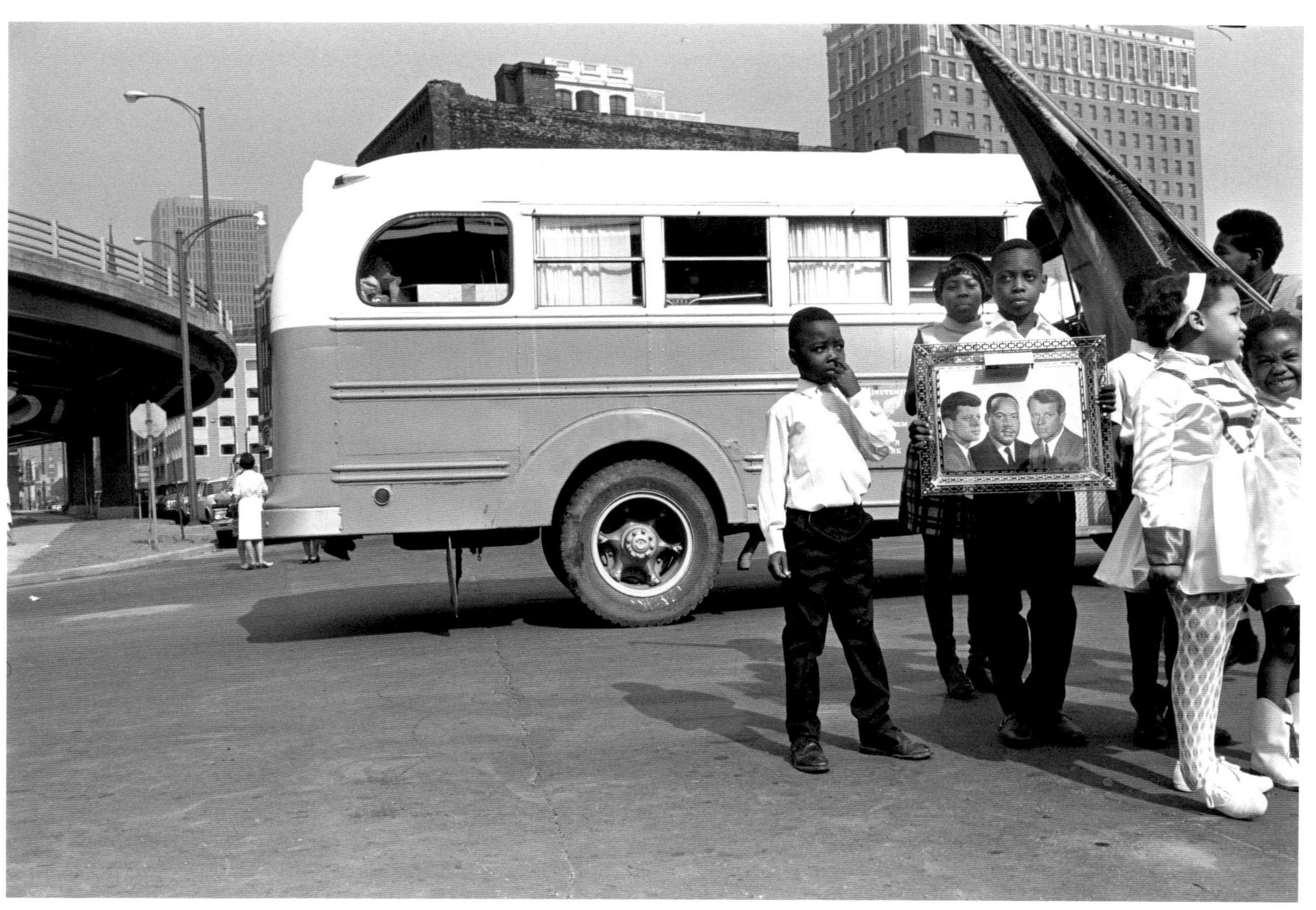

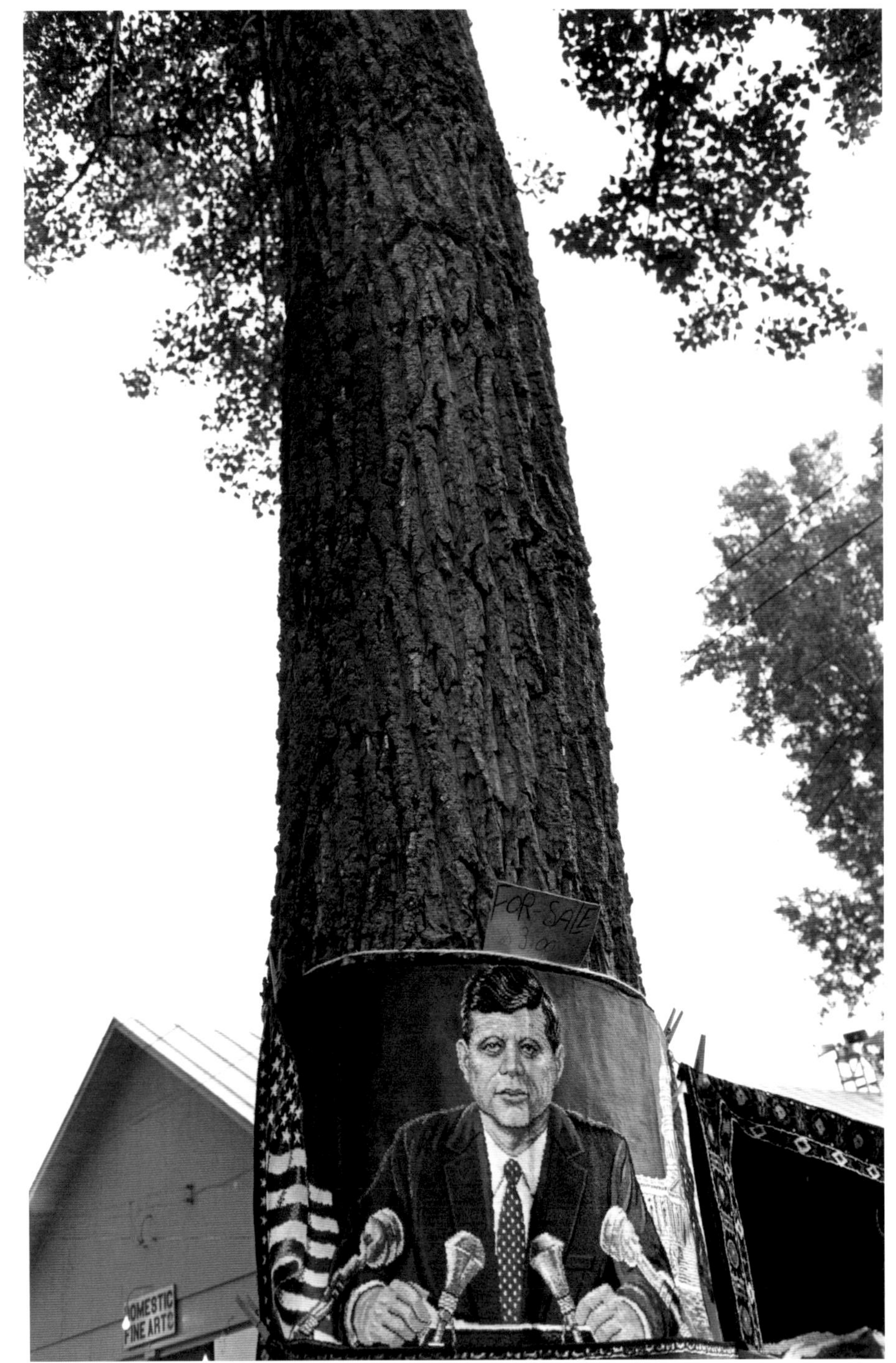
FOR SALE
3.00
DOMESTIC
FINE ARTS

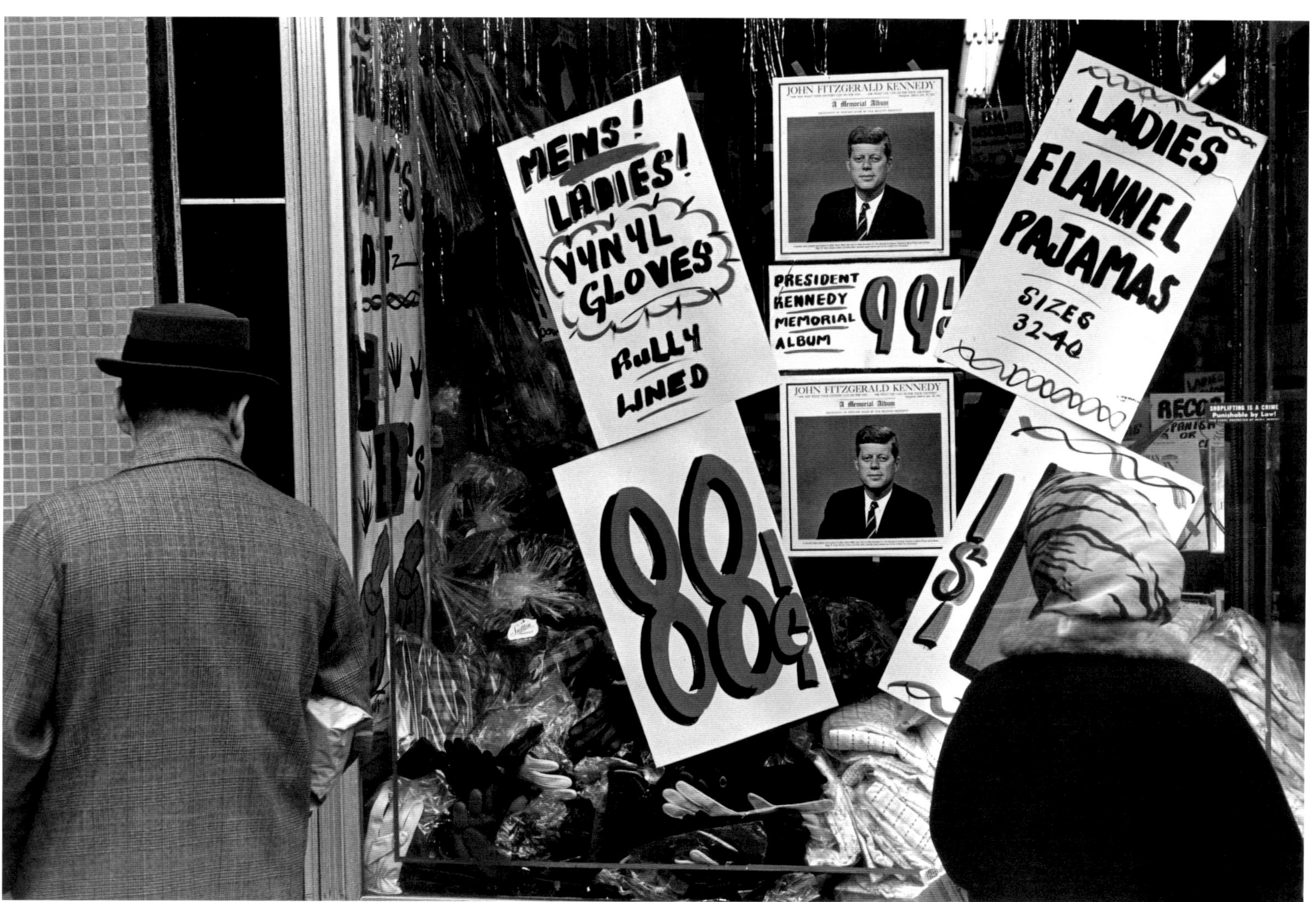
MENS!
LADIES!
VYNYL GLOVES
FULLY LINED
PRESIDENT KENNEDY MEMORIAL ALBUM
99¢
88¢
$1
LADIES FLANNEL PAJAMAS
SIZES 32-40
JOHN FITZGERALD KENNEDY
A Memorial Album
JOHN FITZGERALD KENNEDY
A Memorial Album
SHOPLIFTING IS A CRIME
Punishable by Law!
RECO

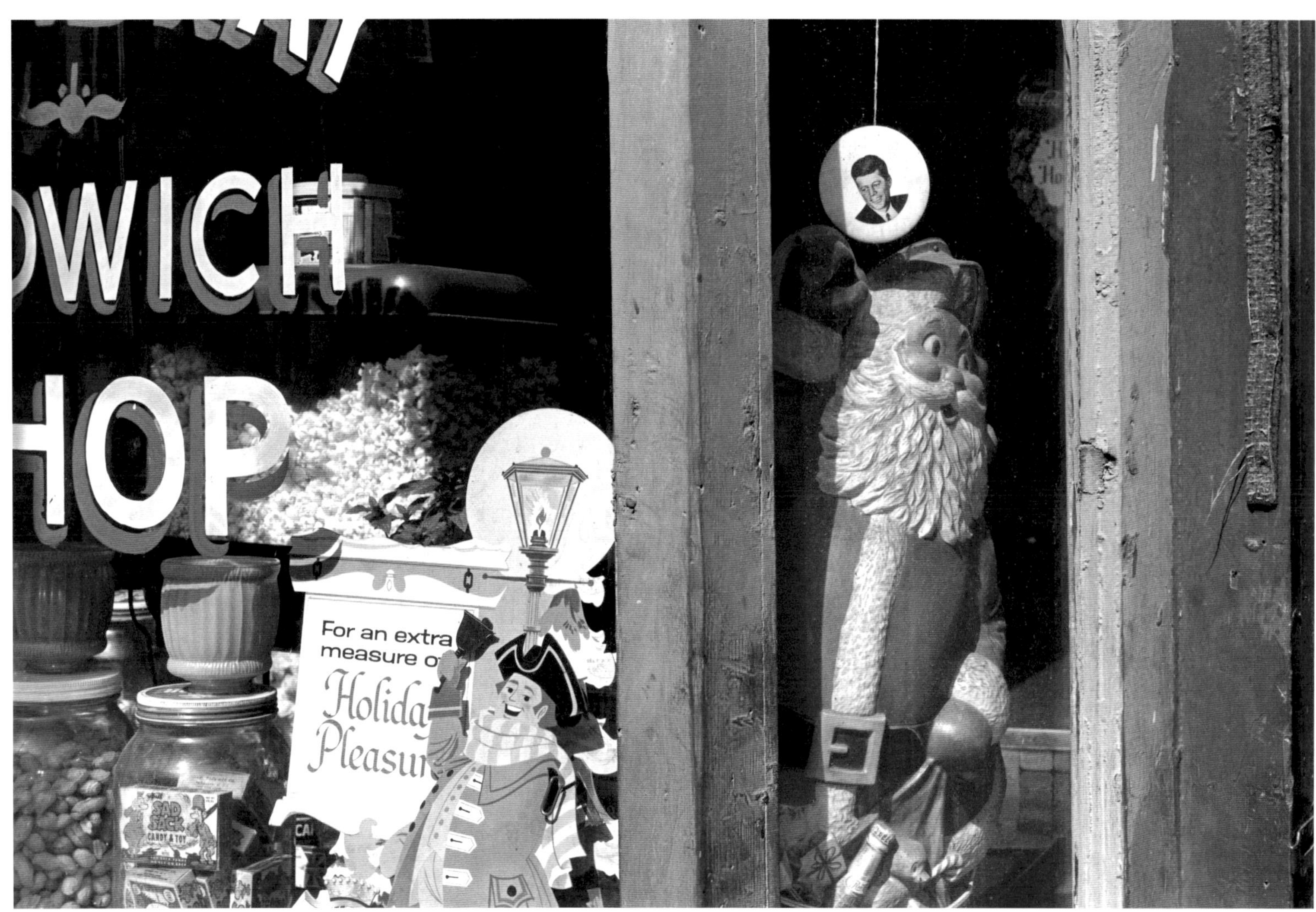
DWICH
HOP
For an extra
measure of
Holiday
Pleasure
SAD
SACK
CANDY & TOY

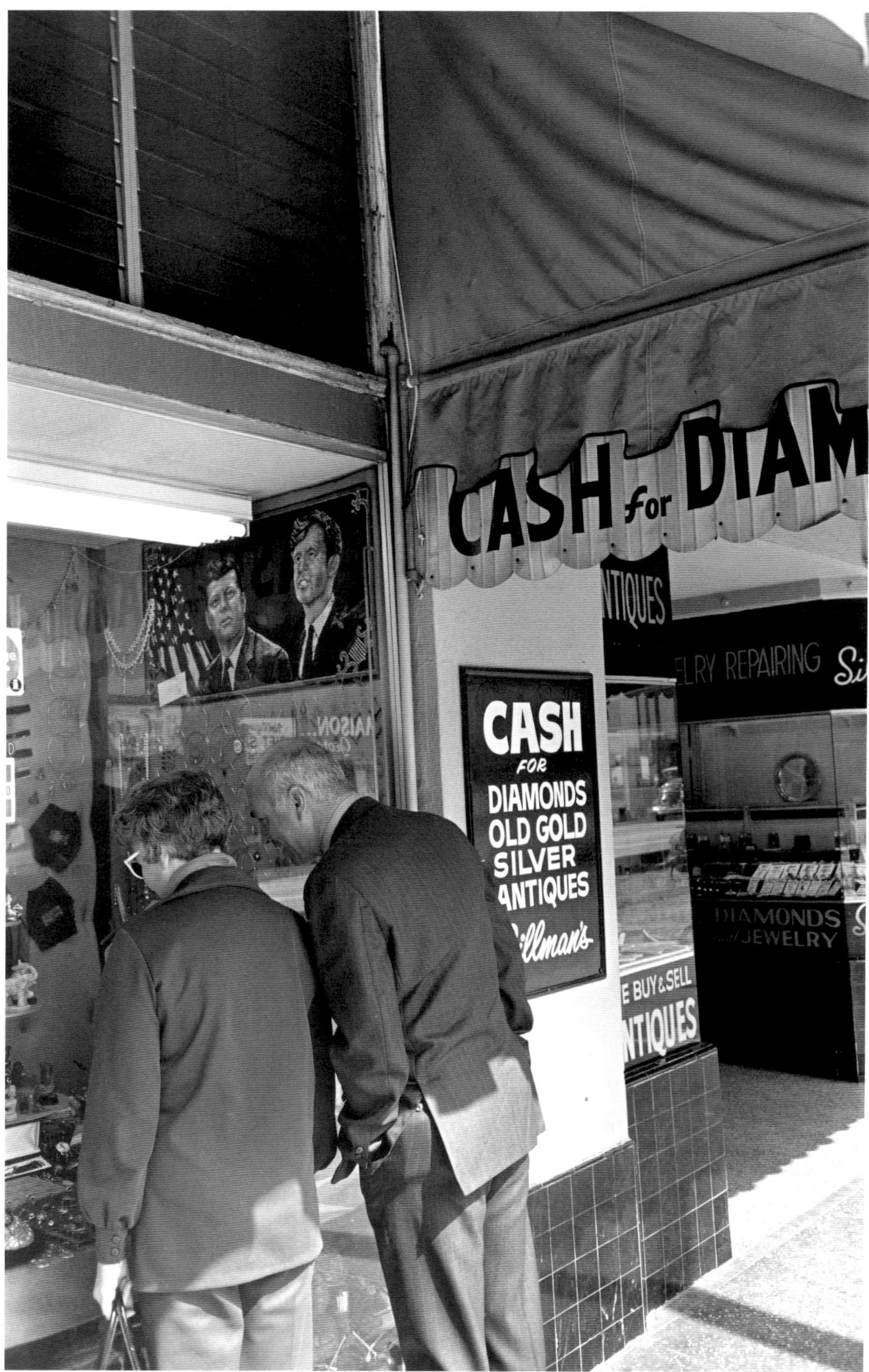

CASH for DIAM
CASH
FOR
DIAMONDS
OLD GOLD
SILVER
ANTIQUES
Tillman's
ANTIQUES
ELRY REPAIRING
DIAMONDS
JEWELRY
E BUY & SELL
ANTIQUES

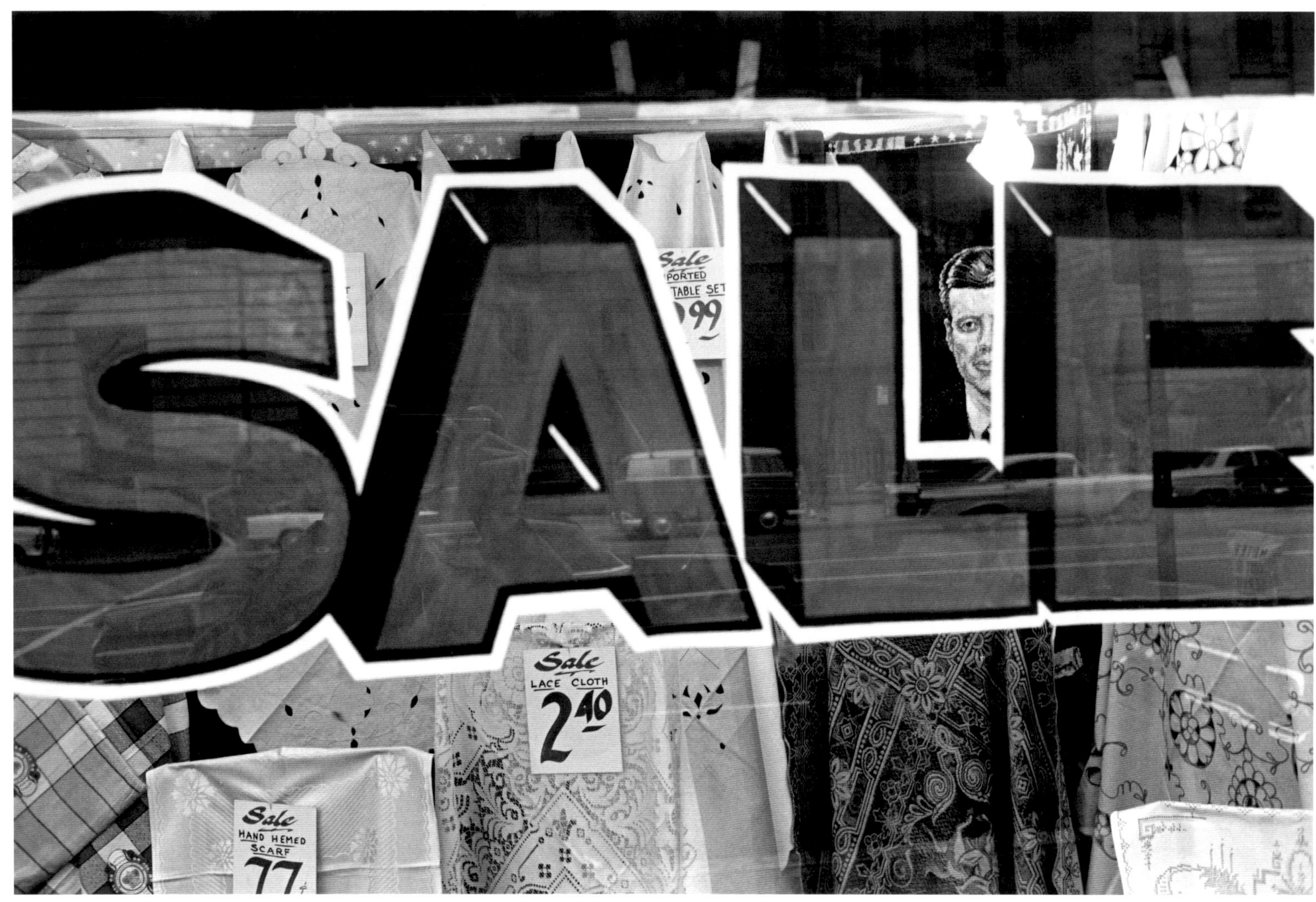
SALE
Sale
IMPORTED
TABLE SET
99
Sale
LACE CLOTH
2 40
Sale
HAND HEMED
SCARF
77¢

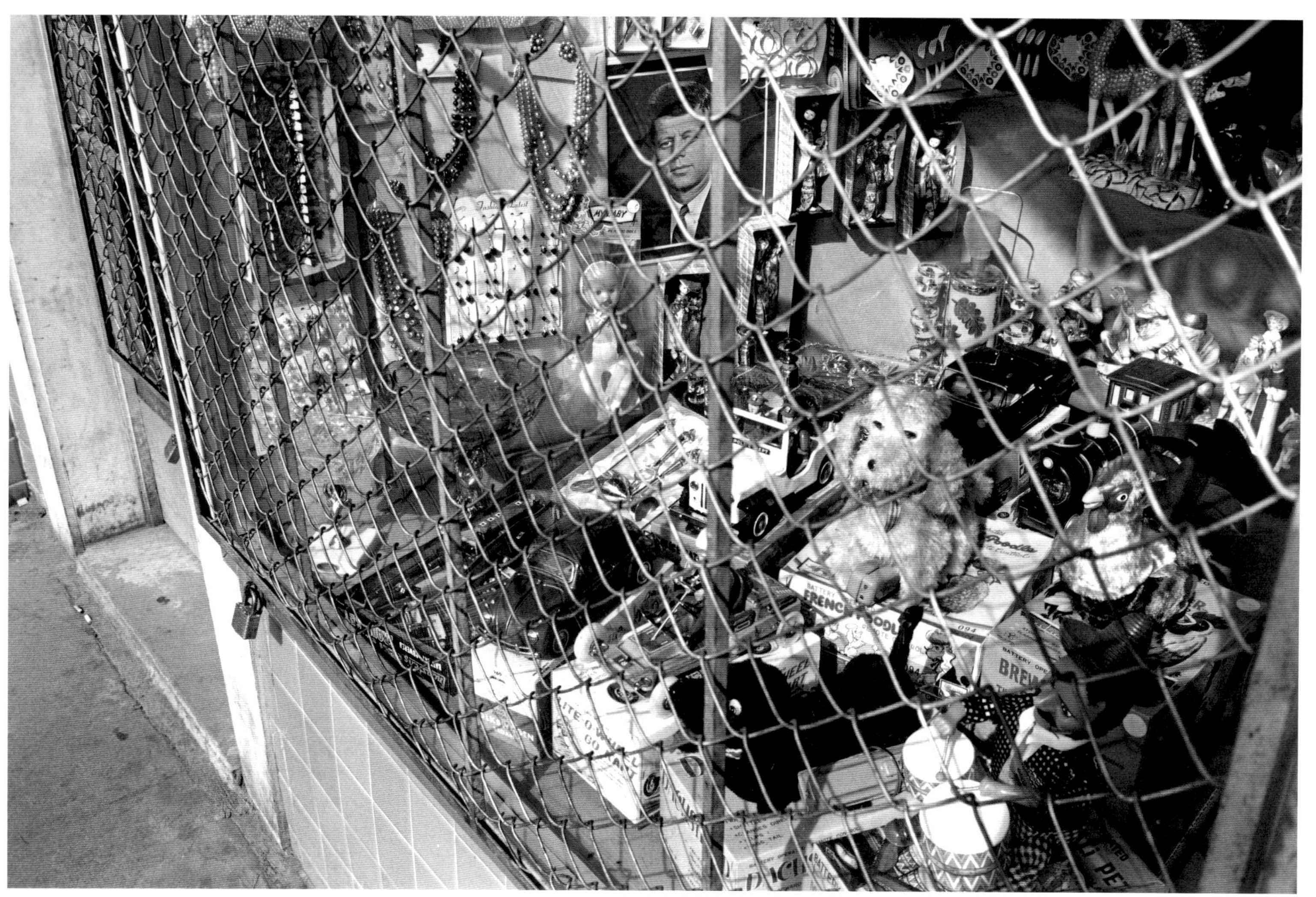

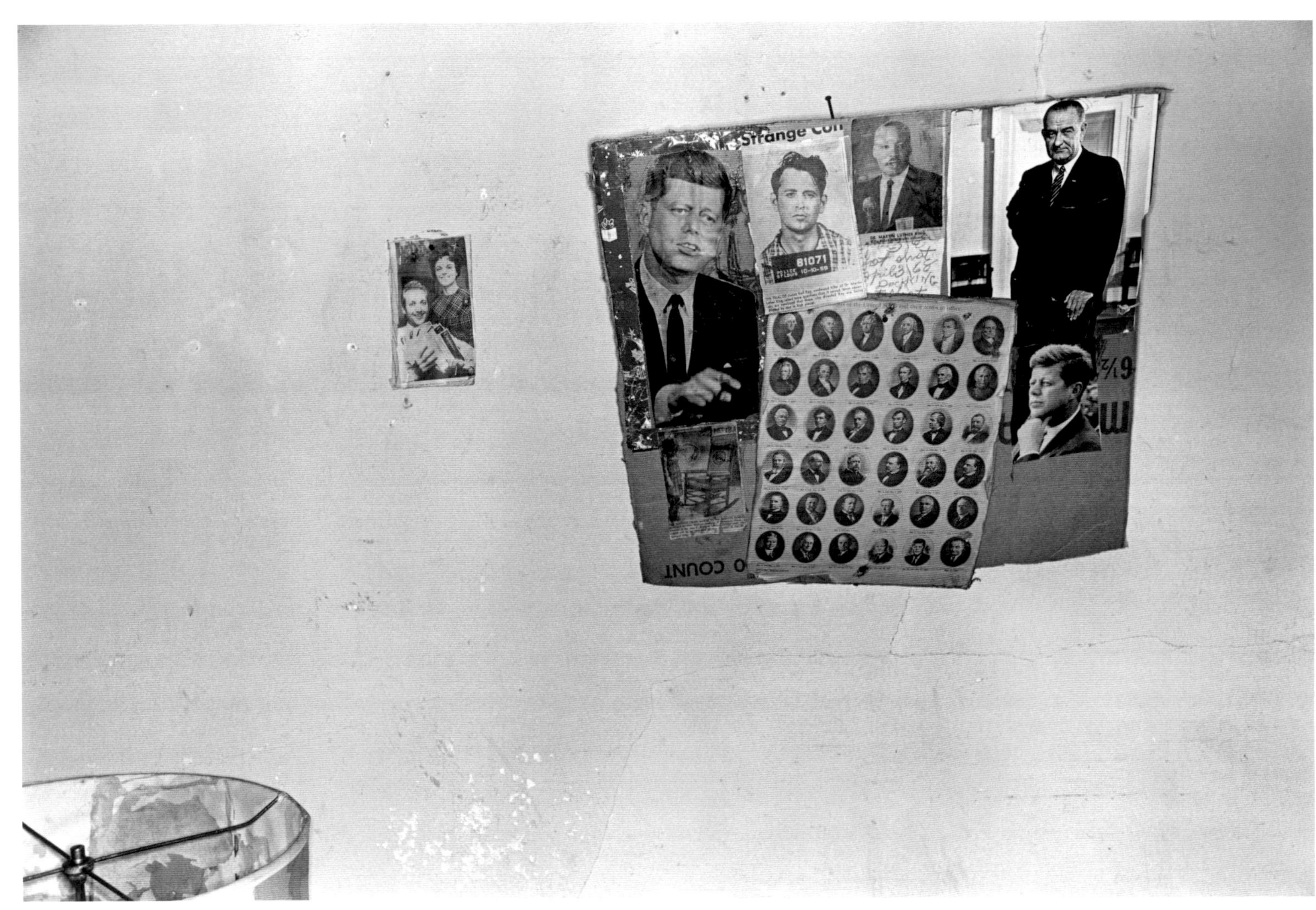

JOHN KENNEDY
OUR NEW
SCHUMANN'S
I'VE BEEN TO
WILDWOOD CREST N.J.
MASS

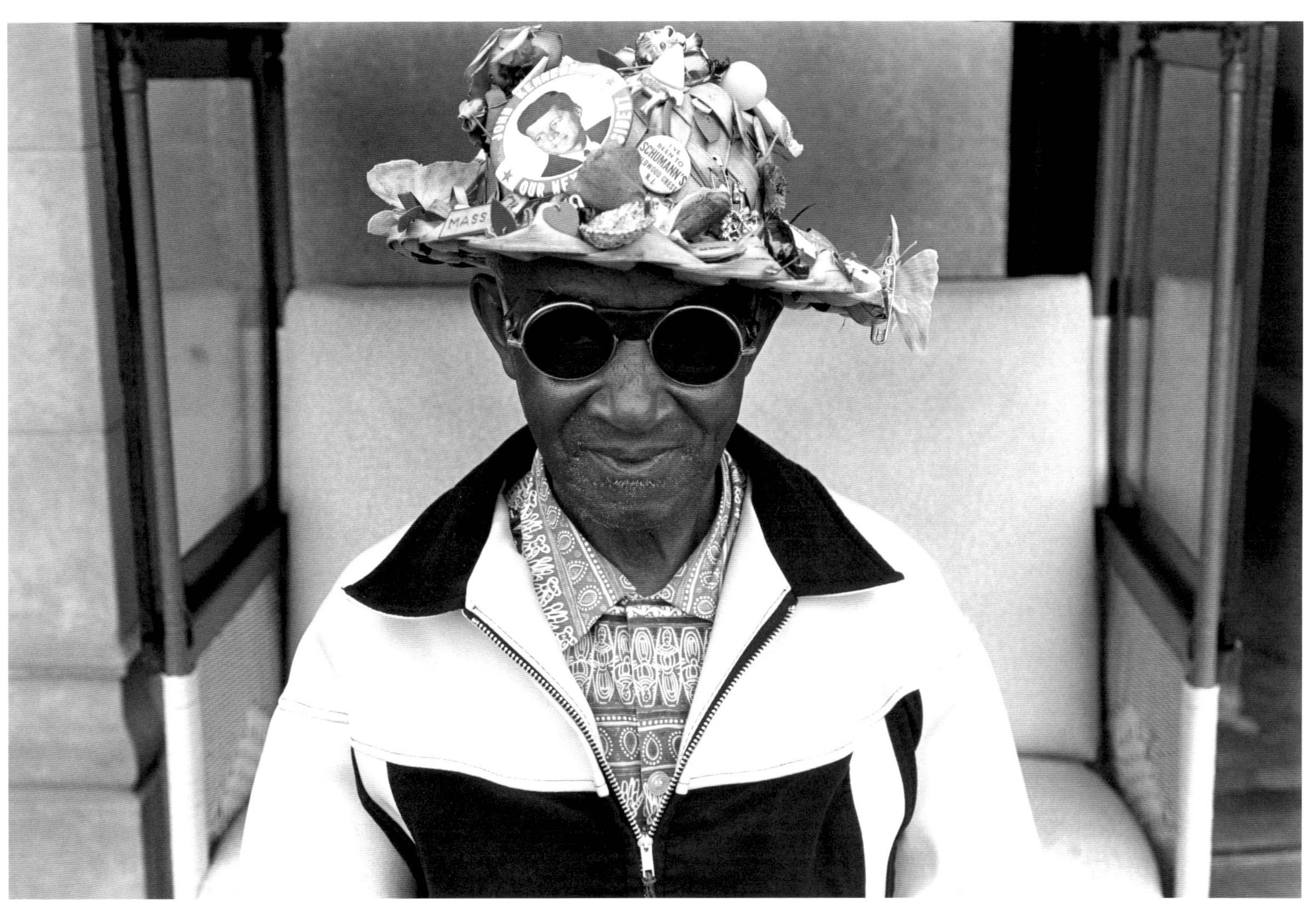

25

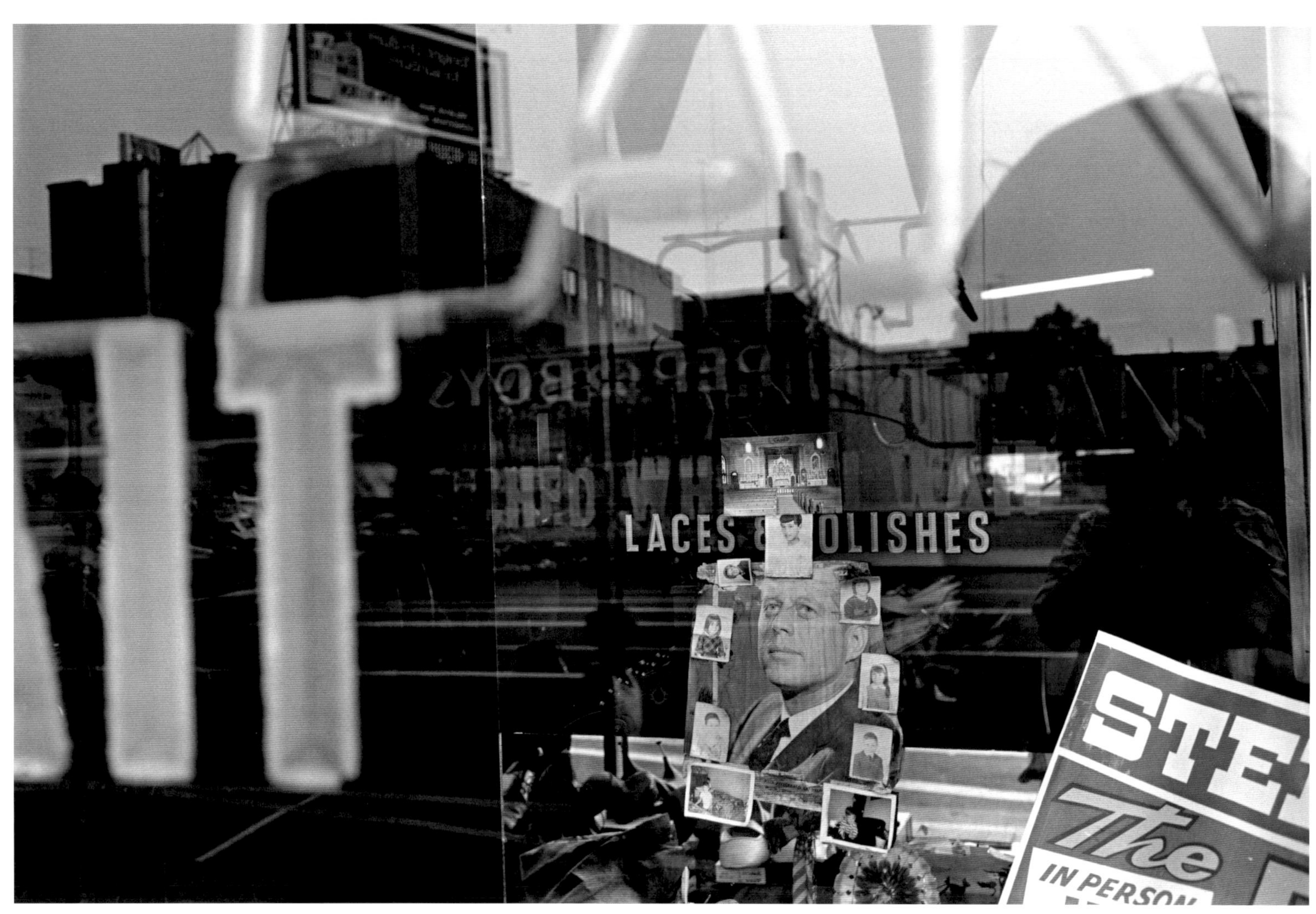
LACES & POLISHES
PEP BOYS
STE
The
IN PERSON

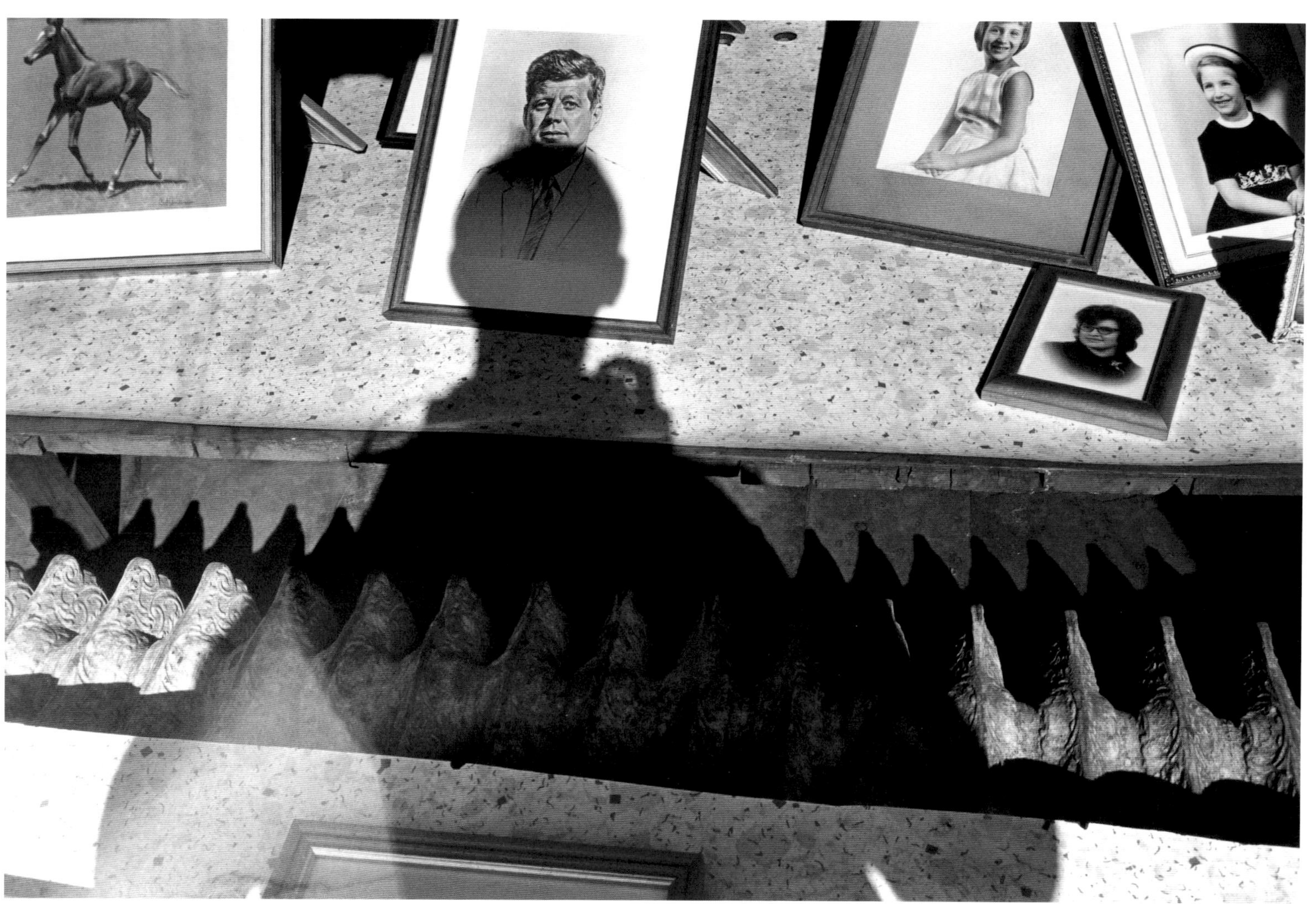

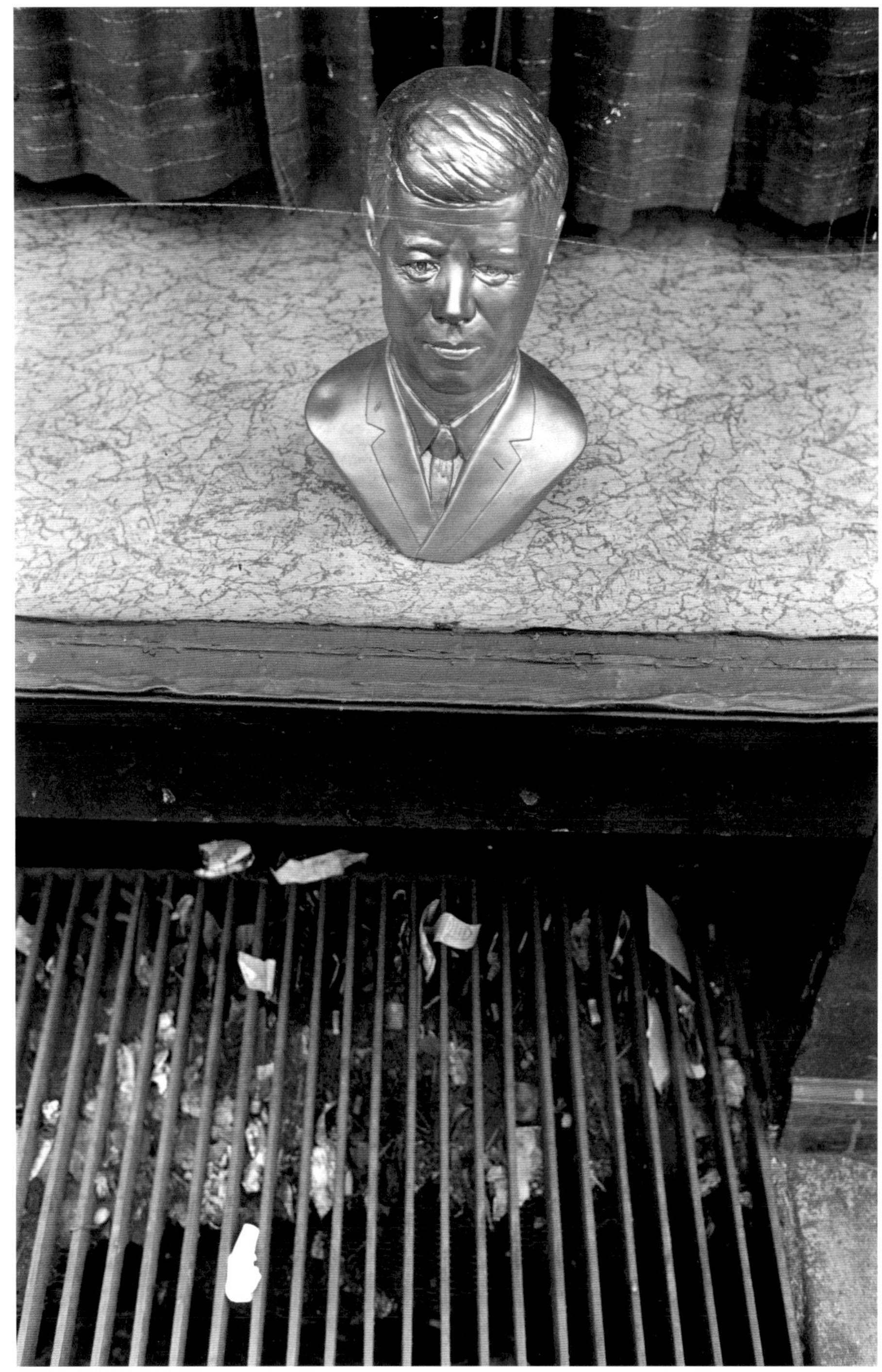

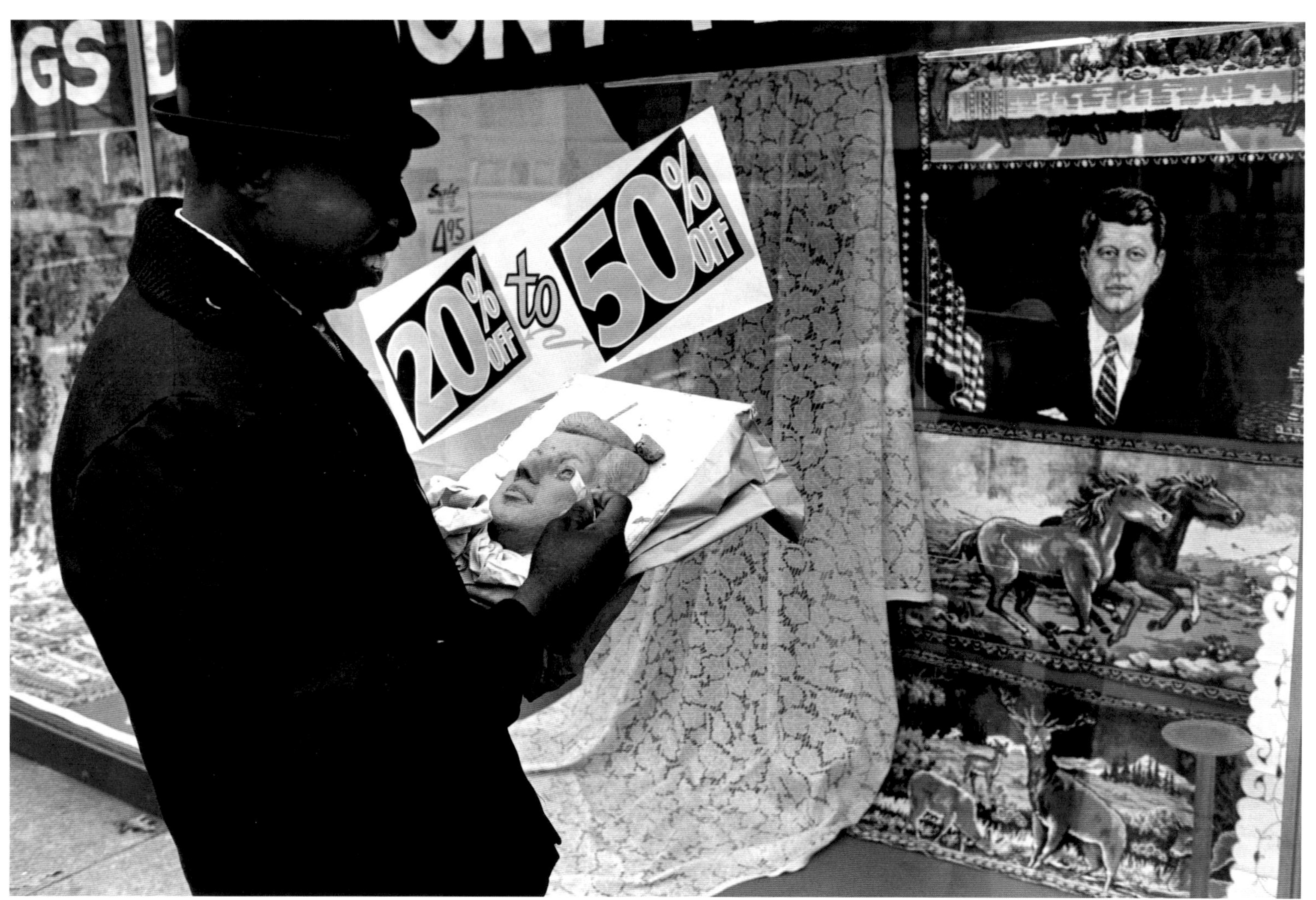
GS D
20% OFF to 50% OFF

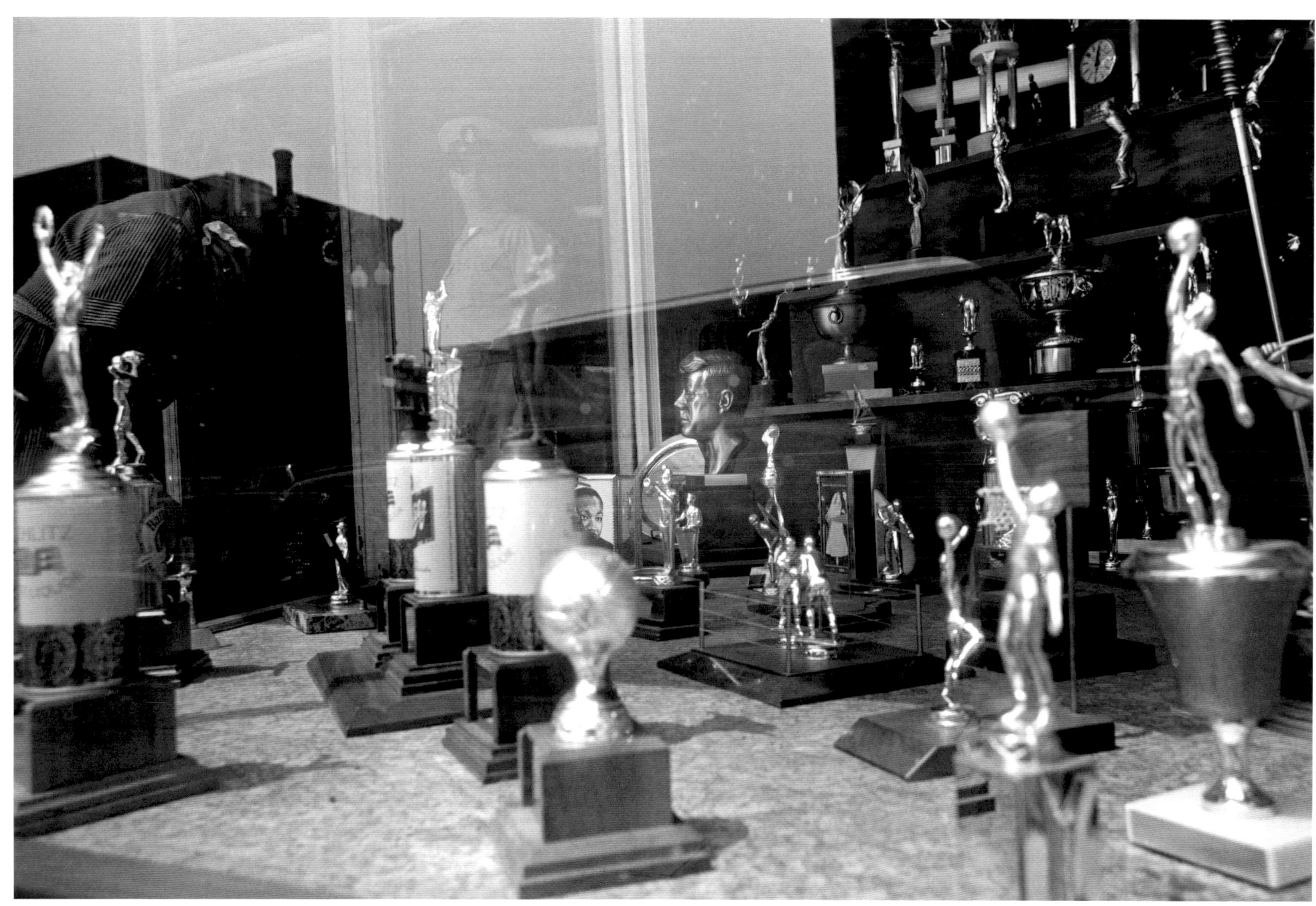

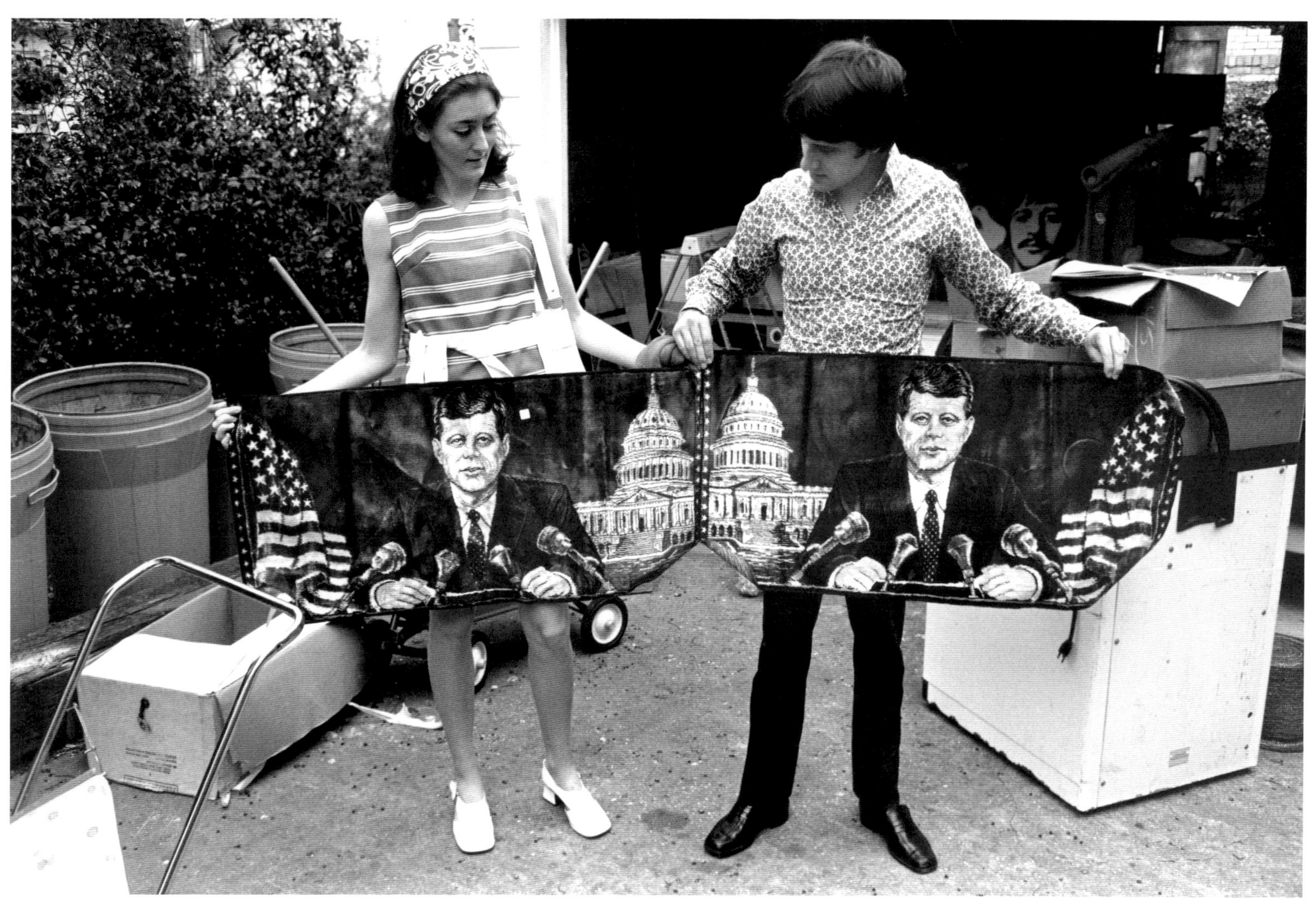

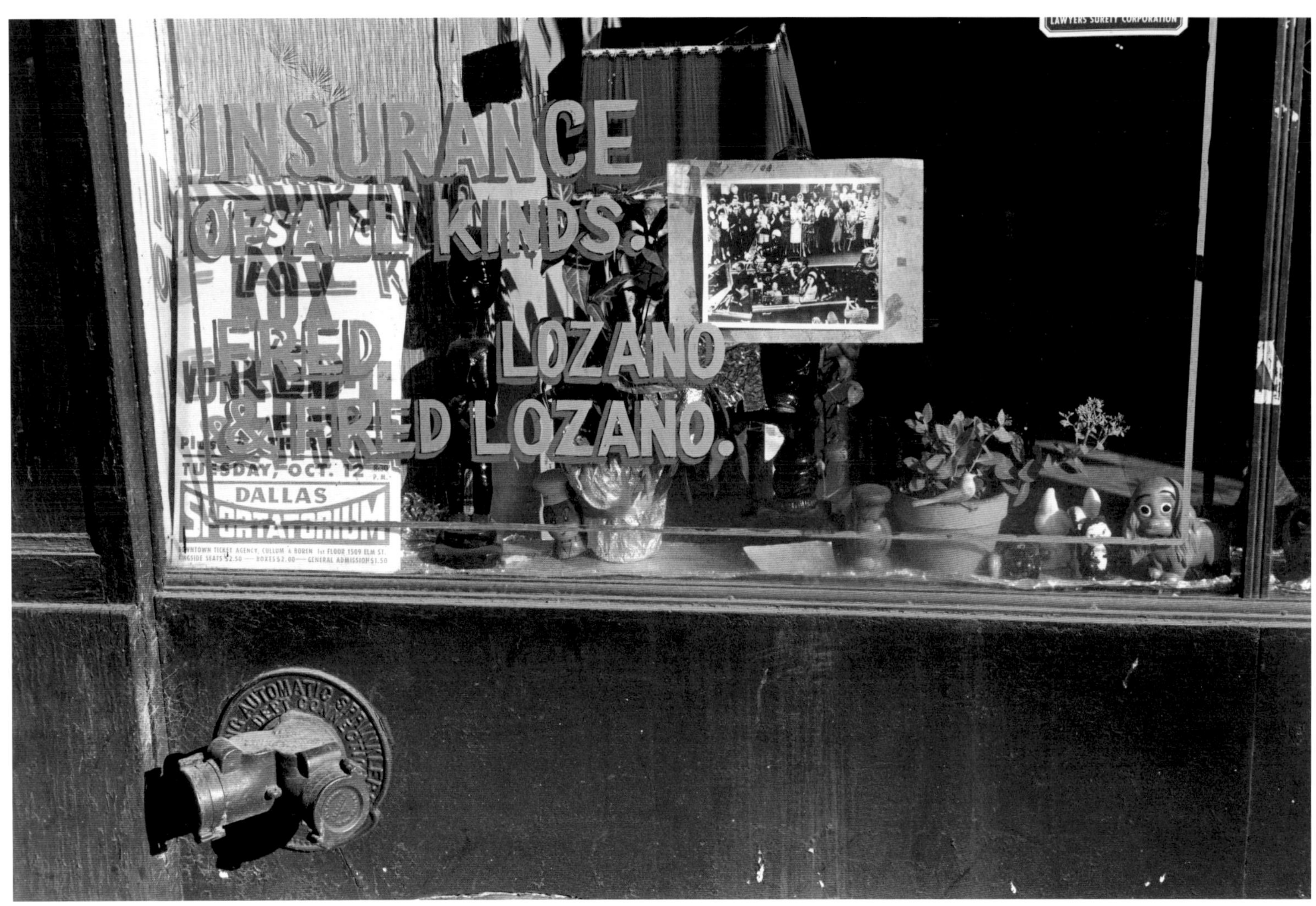

LAWYERS SURETY CORPORATION
INSURANCE
OF ALL KINDS.
FRED LOZANO
& FRED LOZANO.
TUESDAY, OCT. 12 8:30 P.M.
DALLAS SPORTATORIUM
DOWNTOWN TICKET AGENCY, CULLUM & BOREN 1st FLOOR 1509 ELM ST.
RINGSIDE SEATS $2.50 — BOXES $2.00 — GENERAL ADMISSION $1.50
AUTOMATIC SPRINKLER DEPT CONNECTION

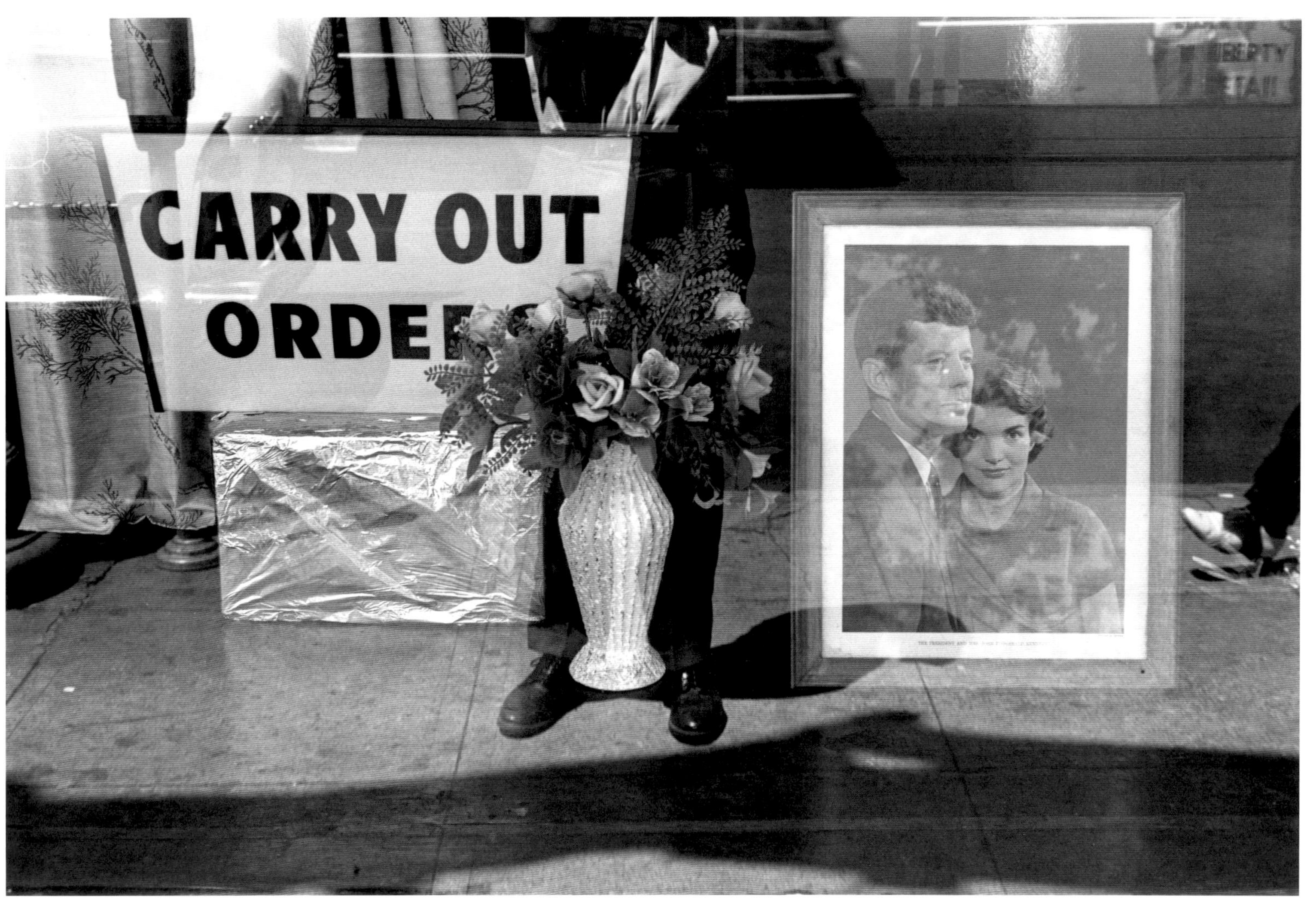

CARRY OUT
ORDERS

The following photographs were made in 1962 at the Columbus Day Parade in Newark, NJ, where JFK addressed the crowd.

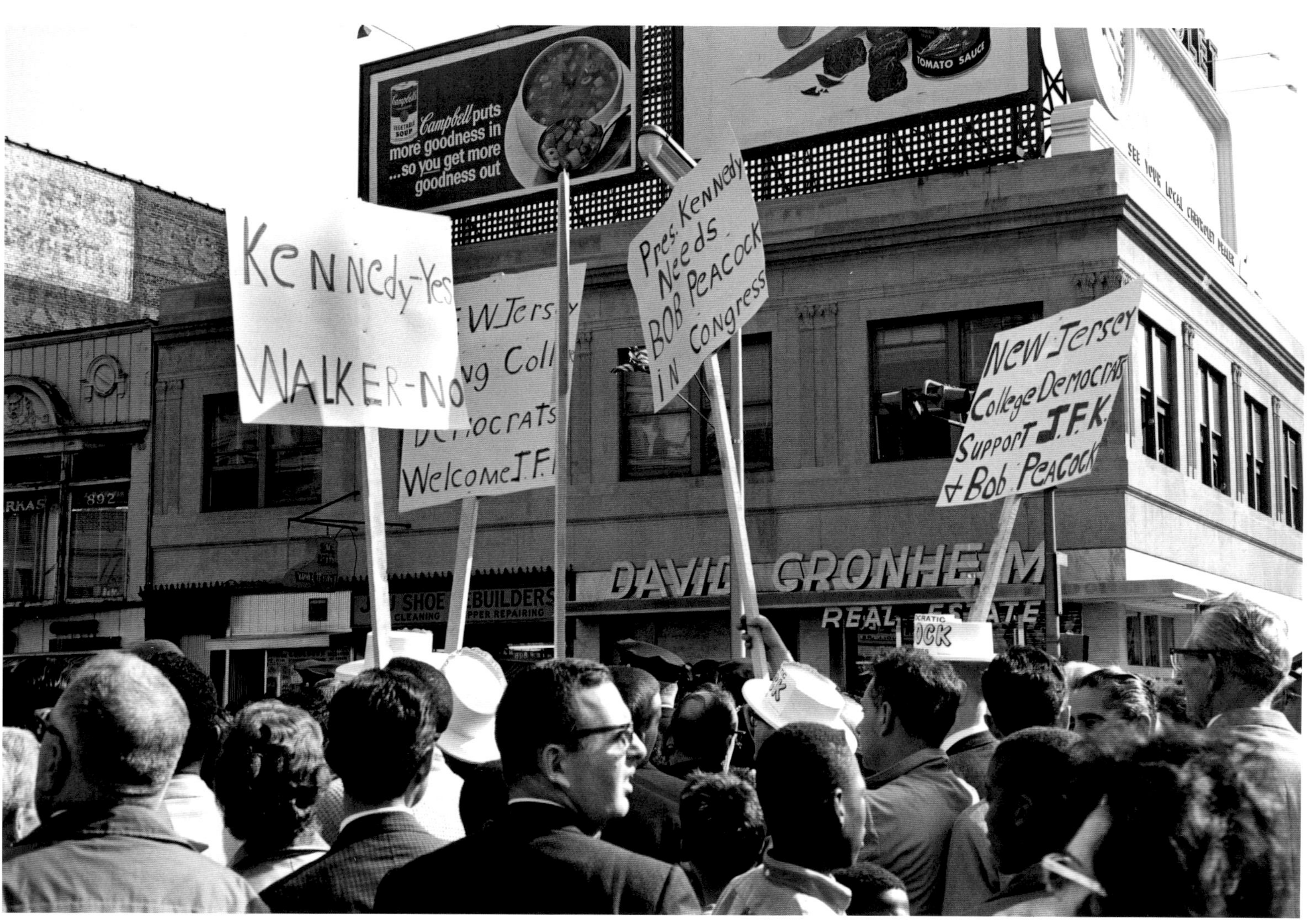
Kennedy-Yes
Walker-No
NEW Jersey
College
Democrats
Welcome J.F.K.
Pres. Kennedy
Needs
BOB Peacock
in Congress
New Jersey
College Democrats
Support J.F.K.
& Bob Peacock
Campbell puts
more goodness in
...so you get more
goodness out
TOMATO SAUCE
SEE YOUR LOCAL CHEVROLET DEALER
DAVID CRONHEIM
REAL ESTATE
SHOE REBUILDERS
CLEANING UPPER REPAIRING
892

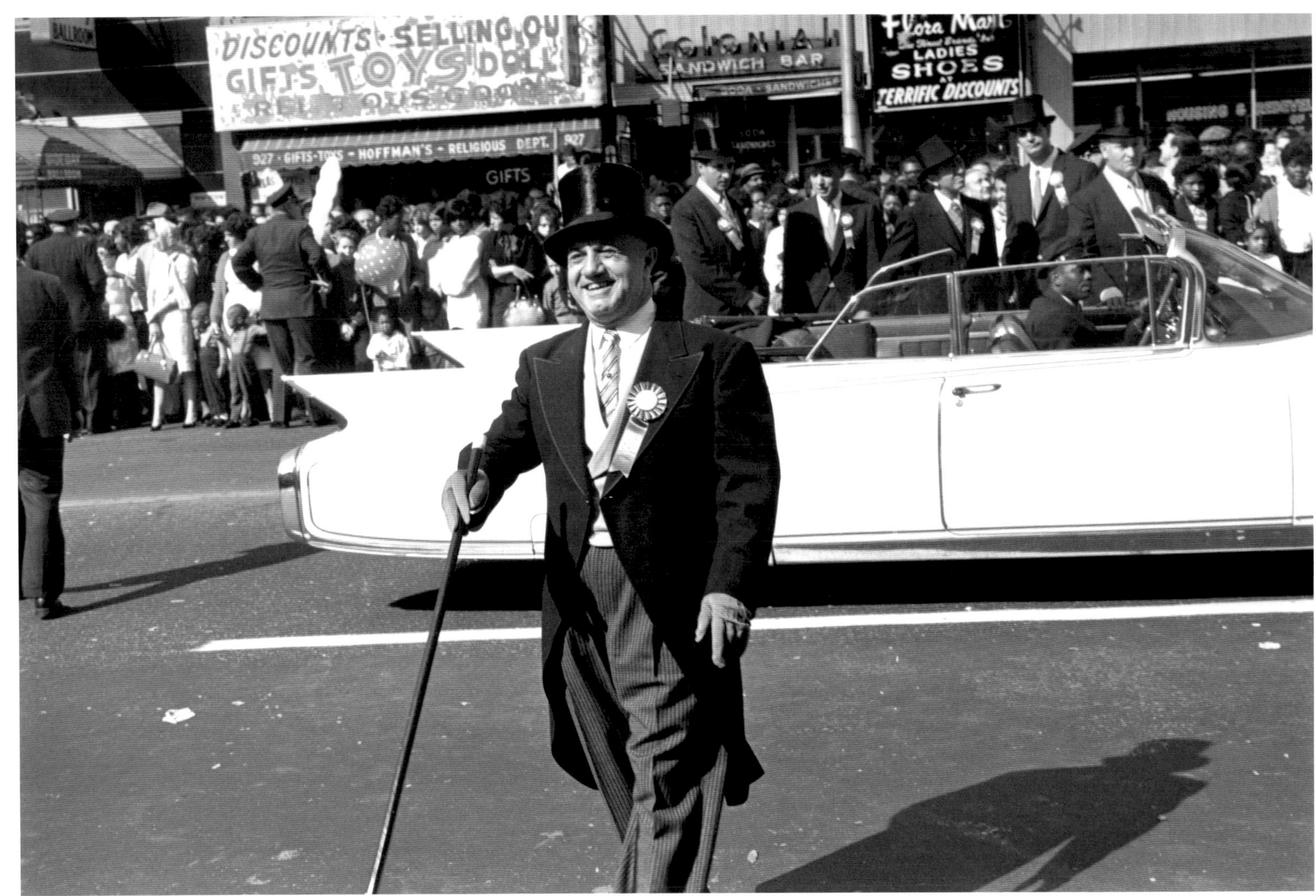
DISCOUNTS · SELLING OU
GIFTS TOYS DOLL
RELIGIOUS
927 · GIFTS·TOYS · HOFFMAN'S · RELIGIOUS DEPT. 927
GIFTS
COLONIAL
SANDWICH BAR
SODA · SANDWICH
Flora Mart
LADIES
SHOES
AT
TERRIFIC DISCOUNTS
HOUSING

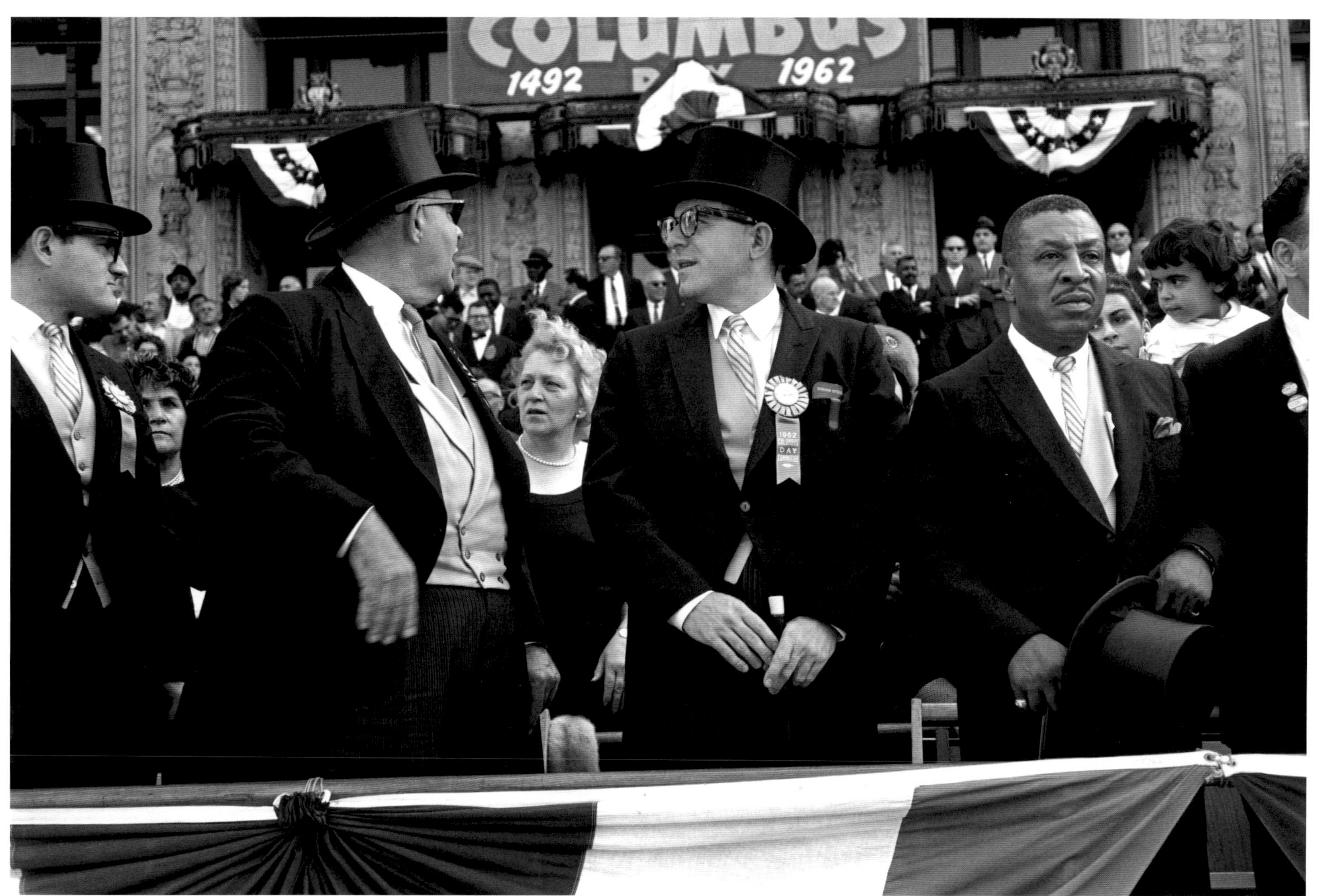
COLUMBUS
1492 1962

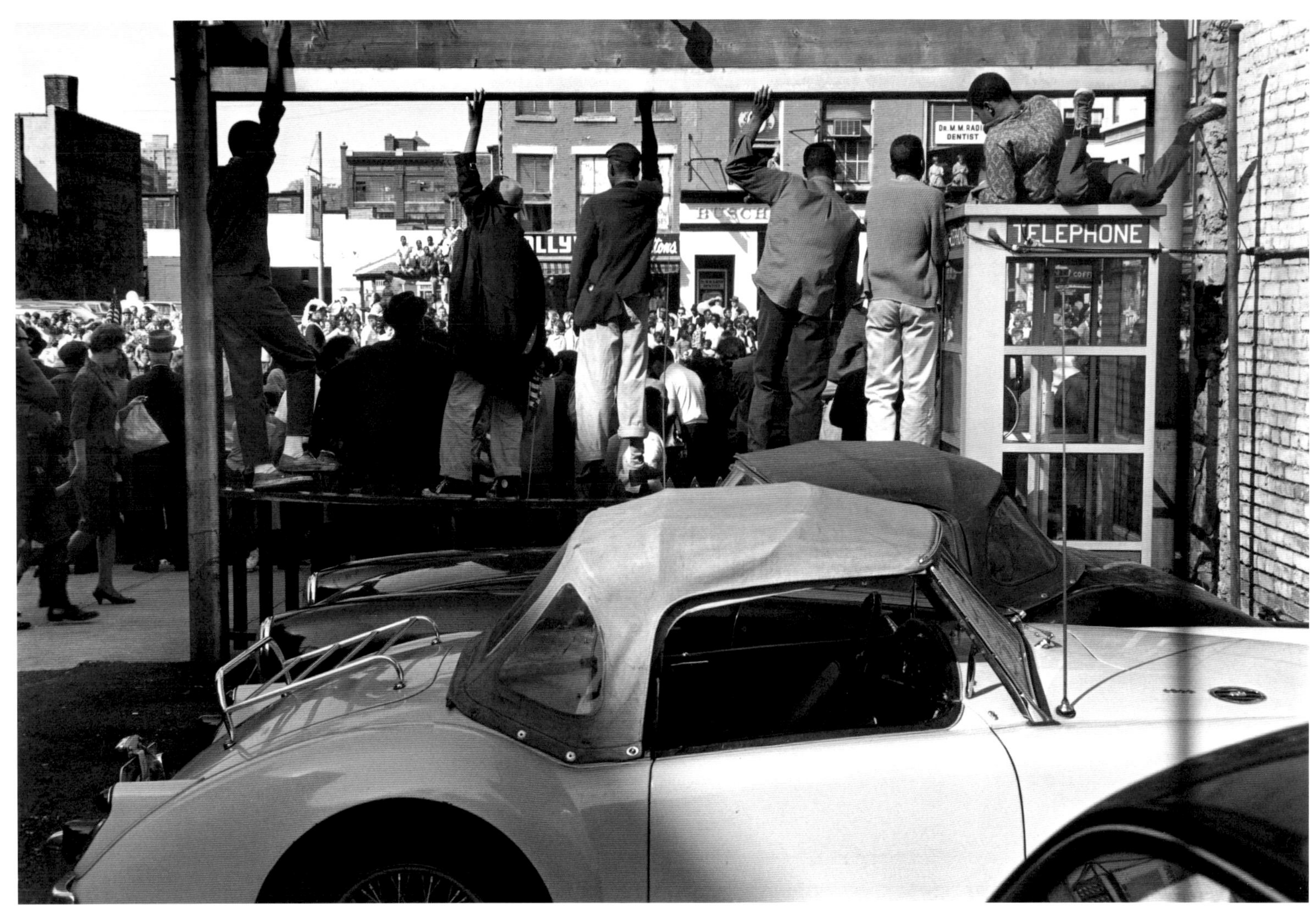

TELEPHONE
Dr. M.M. RAD...
DENTIST
BUSCH

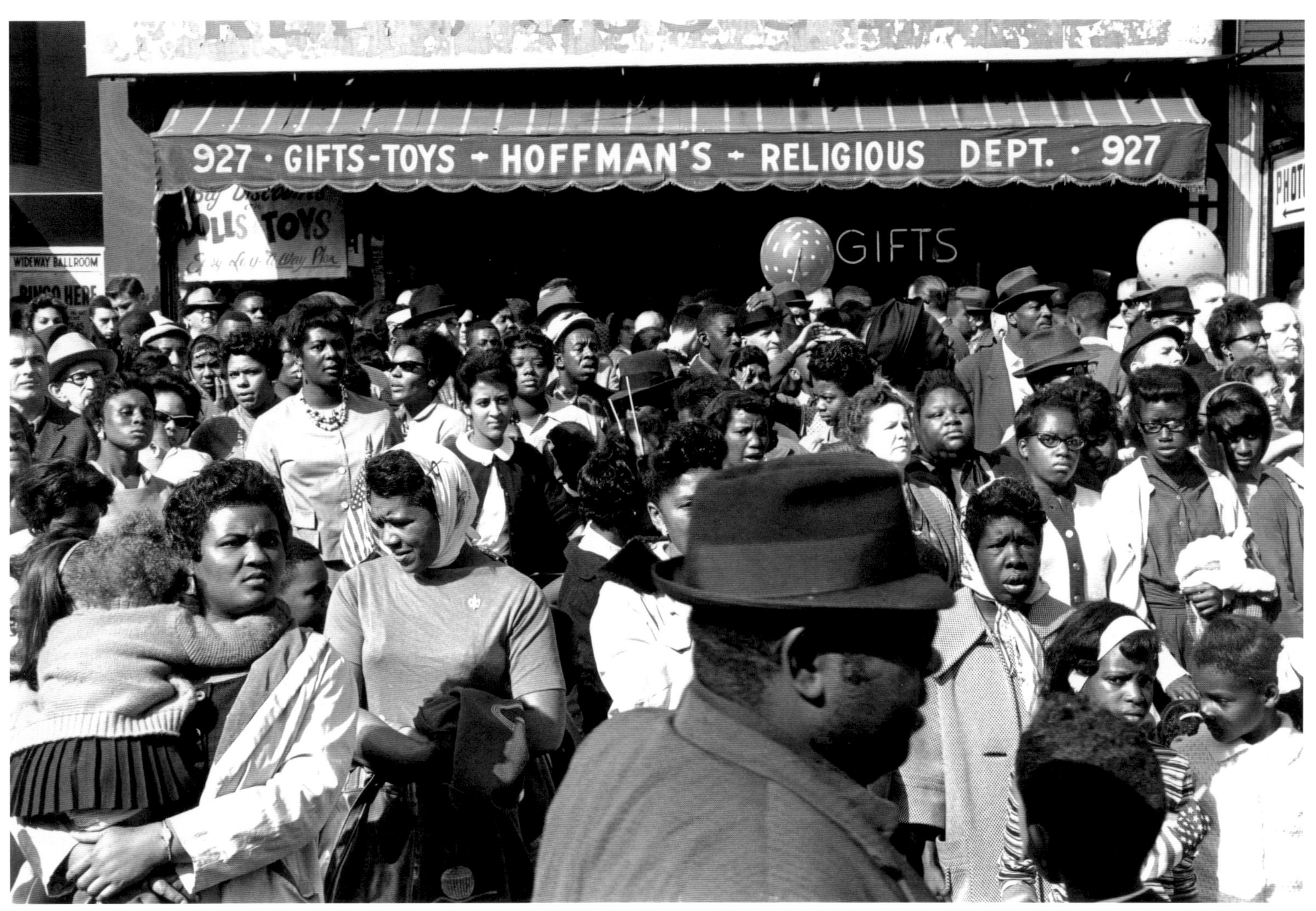
927 · GIFTS-TOYS + HOFFMAN'S + RELIGIOUS DEPT. · 927
GIFTS
DOLLS TOYS
WIDEWAY BALLROOM
BINGO HERE
PHOTO

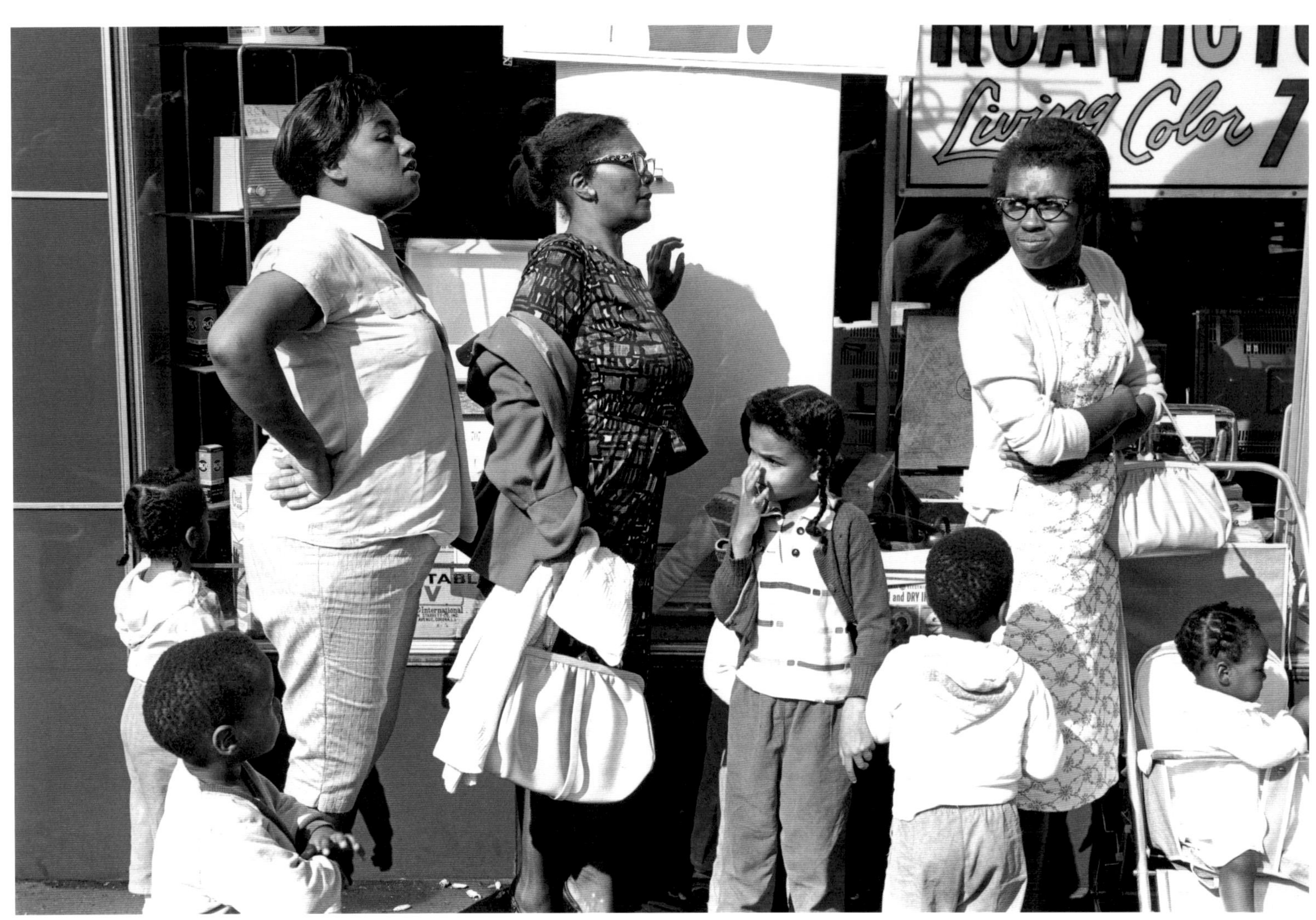

RCA VIC
Living Color 7

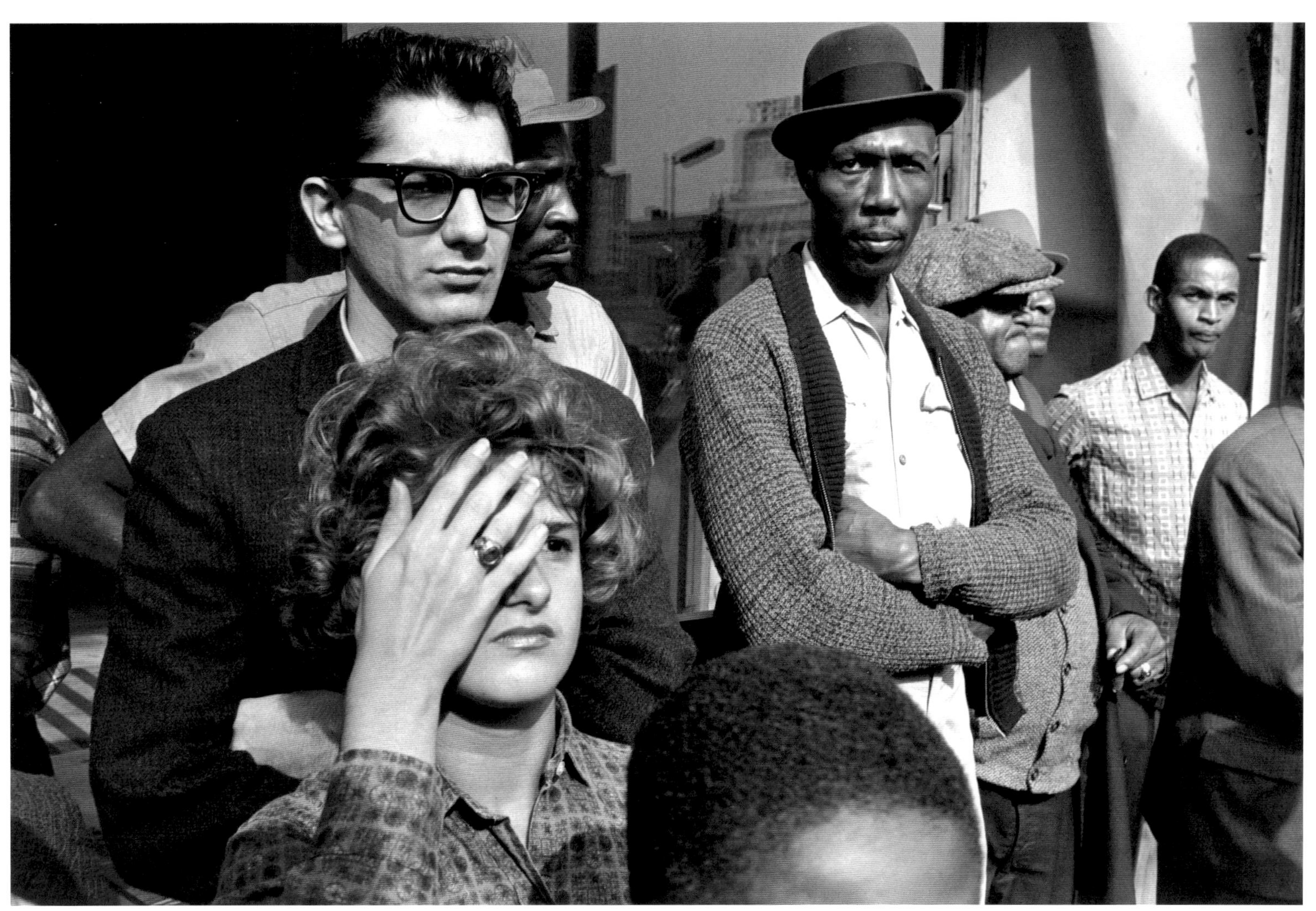

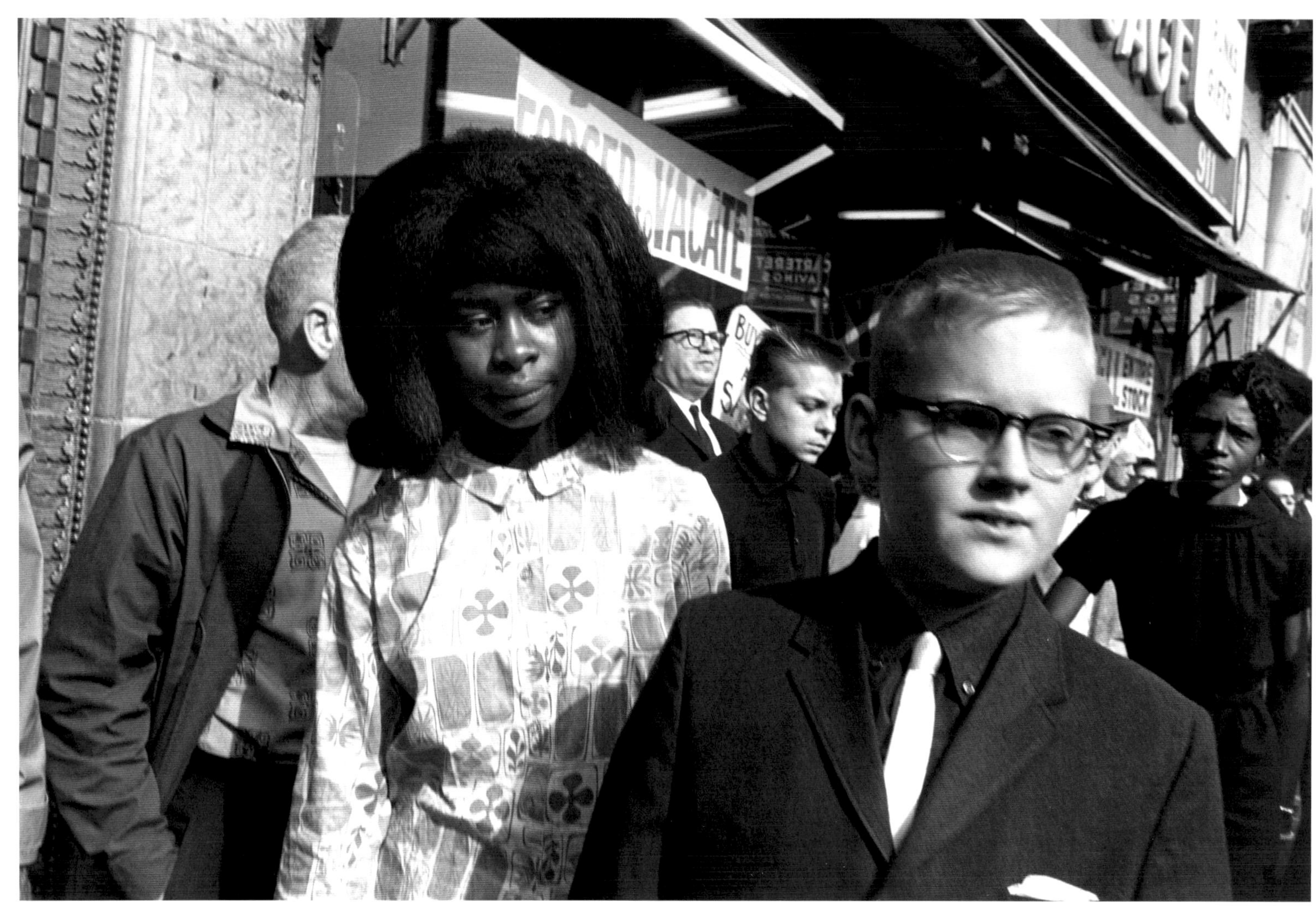

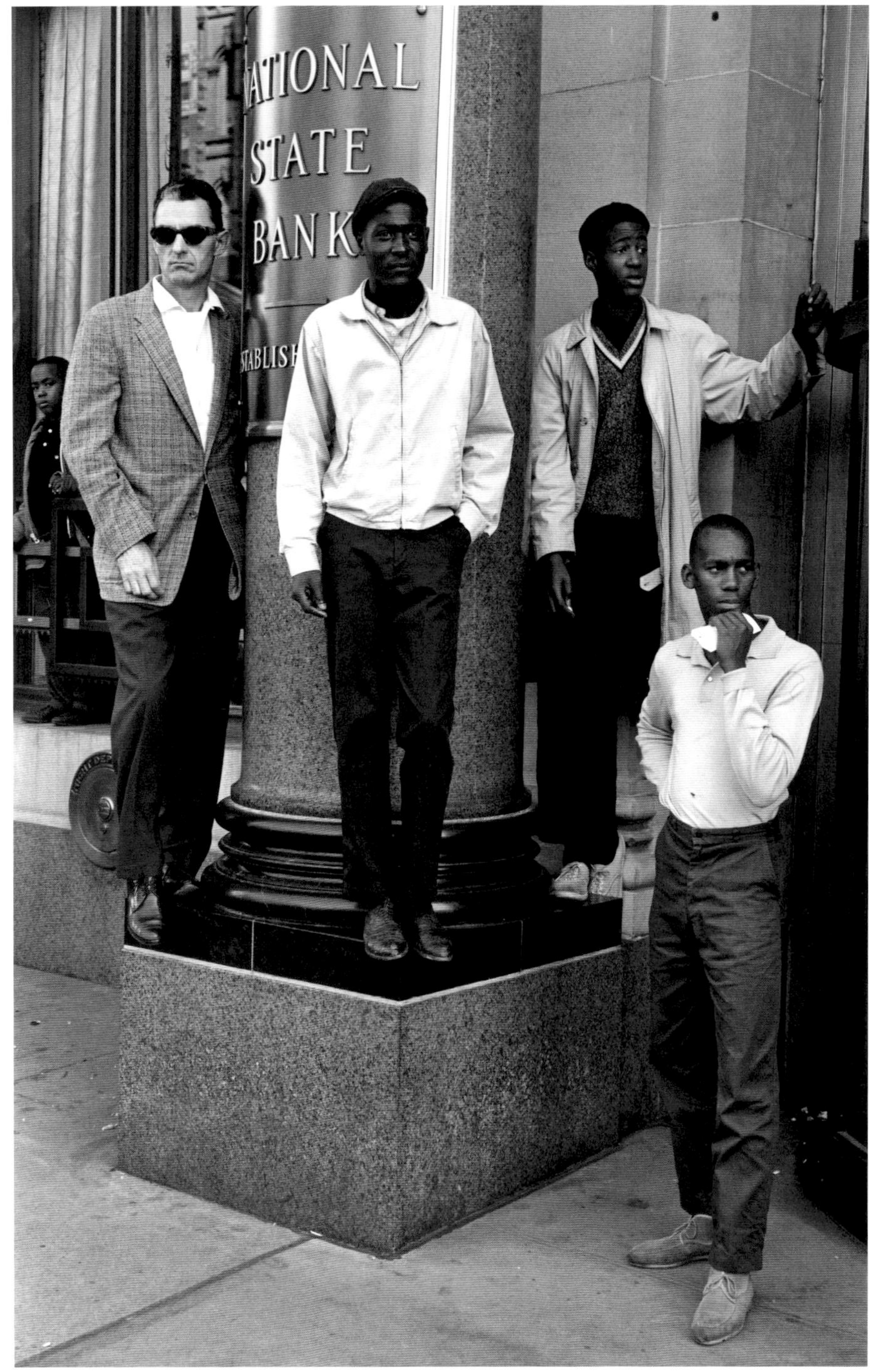

ATIONAL
STATE
BANK
ESTABLISH

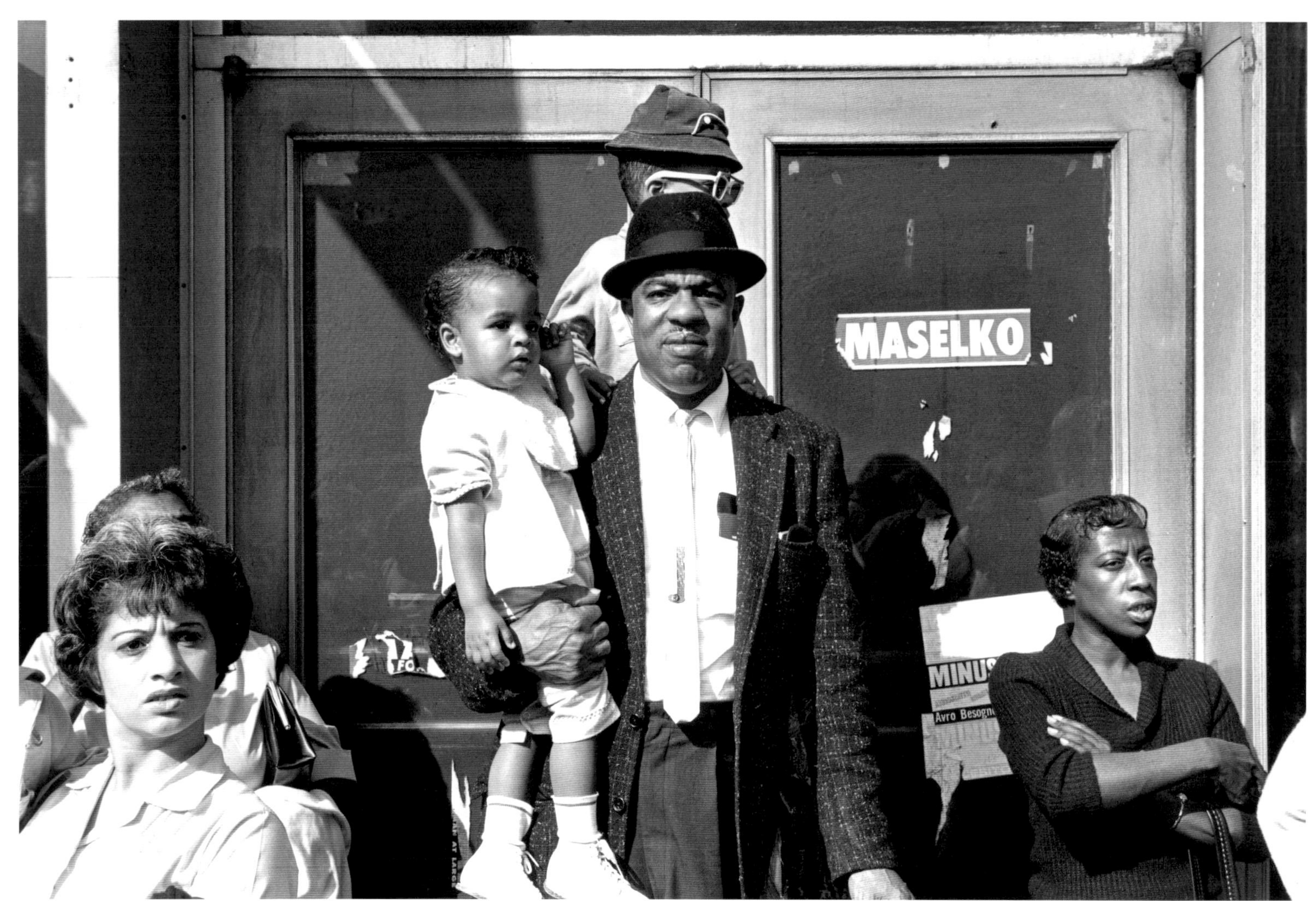
MASELKO
MINUS
Avro Besogn

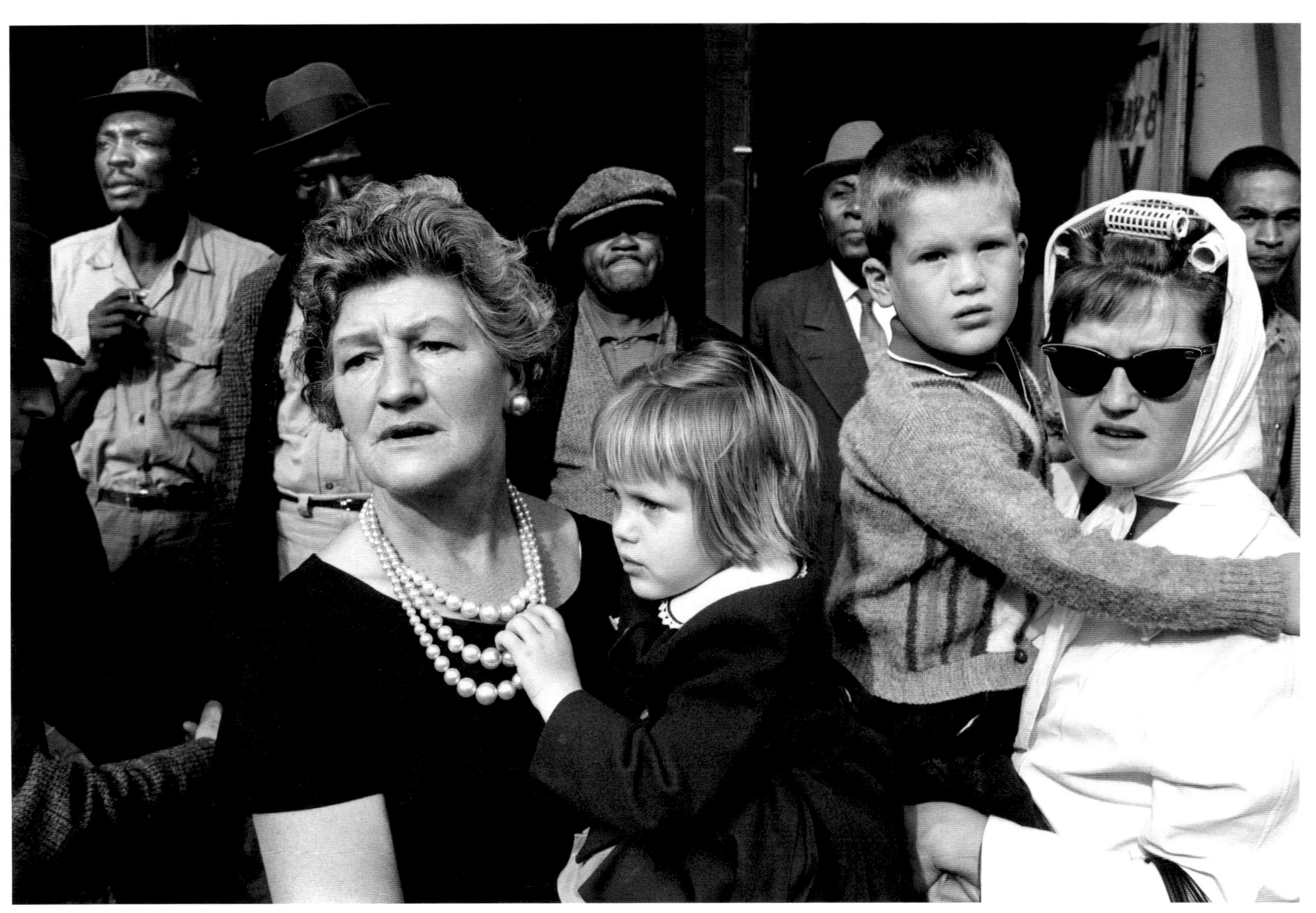

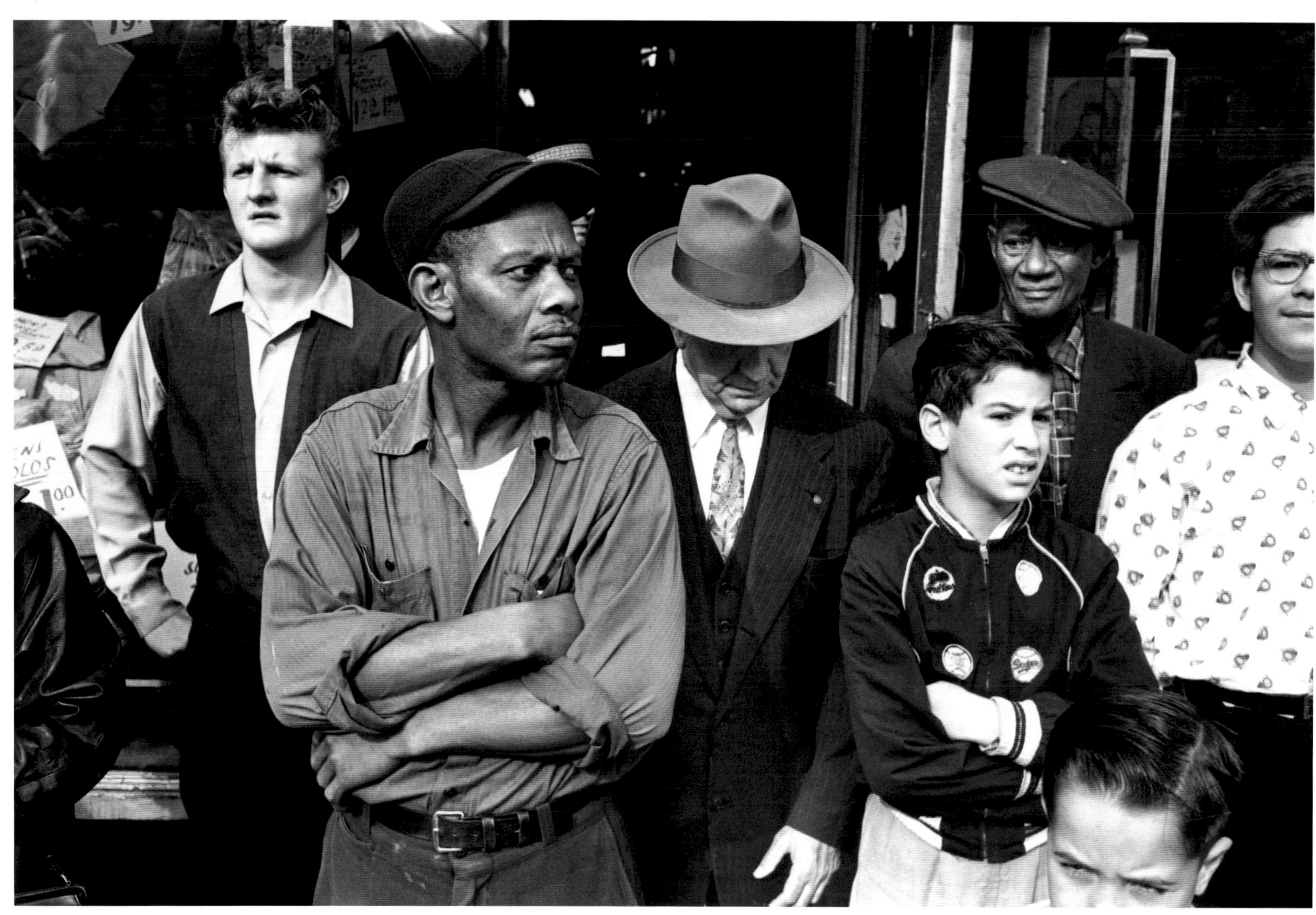

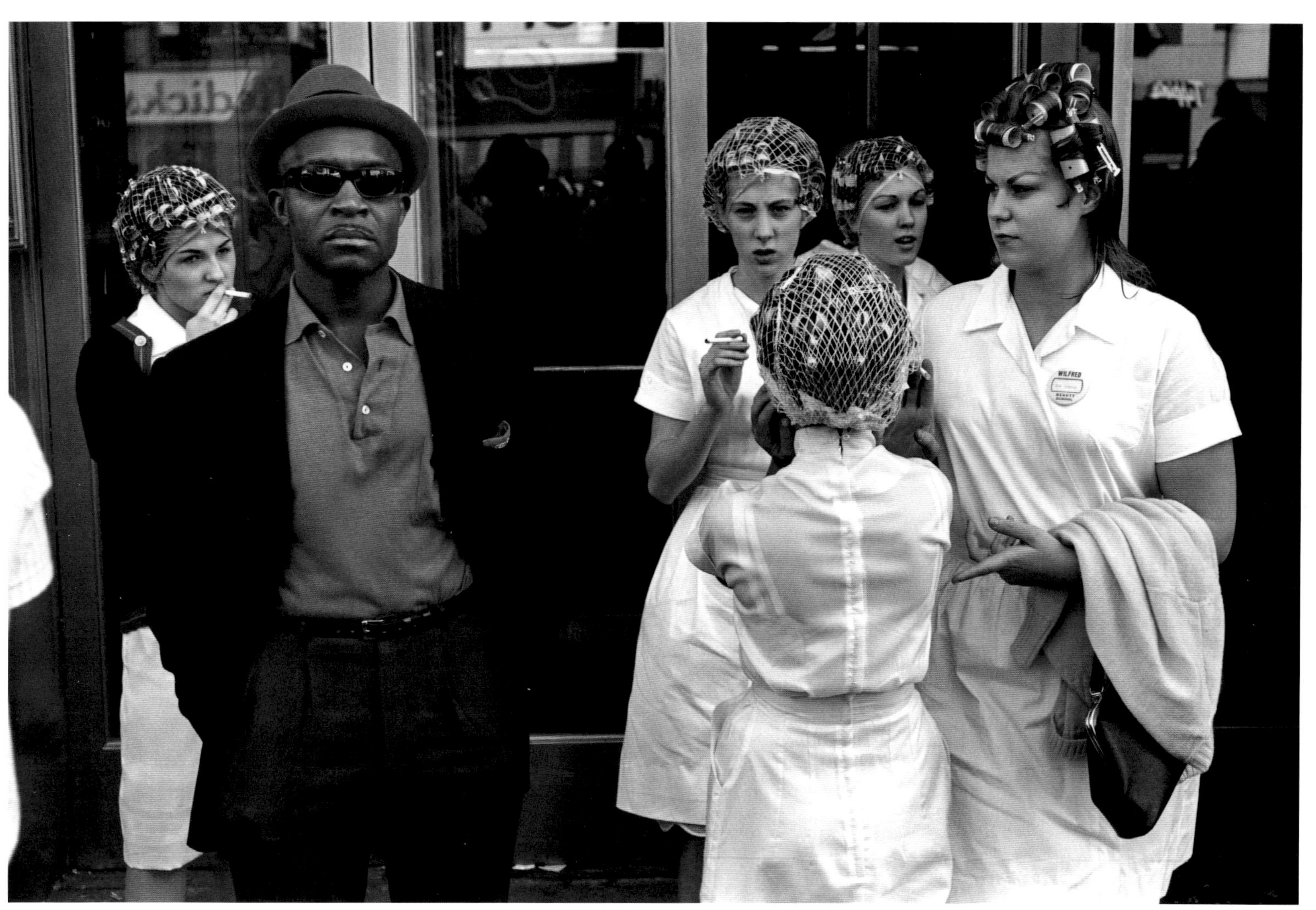

WILFRED
BEAUTY
SCHOOL

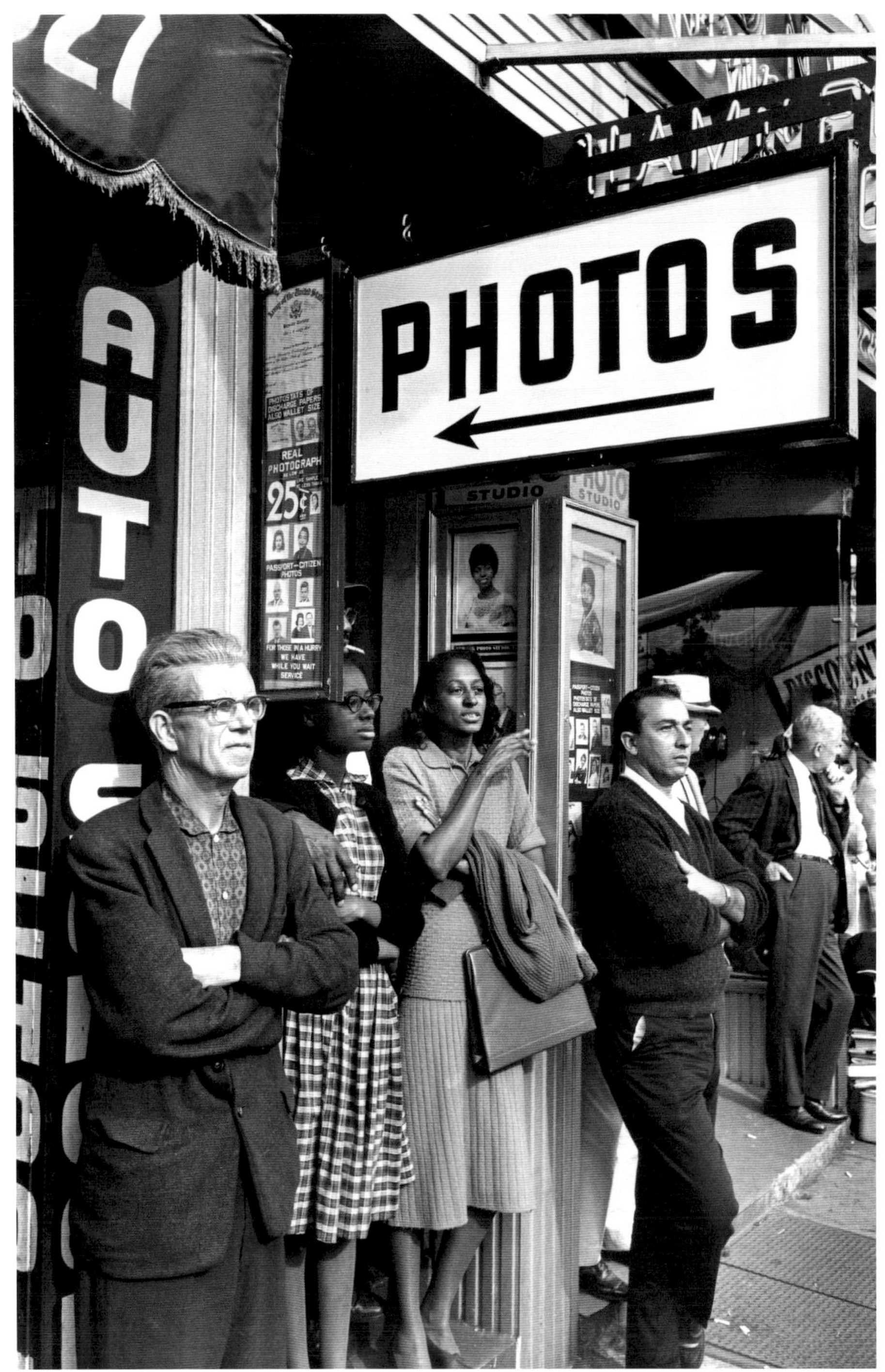
PHOTOS
AUTO
STUDIO
PHOTO STUDIO
REAL
PHOTOGRAPH
25¢
PASSPORT and CITIZEN
PHOTOS
FOR THOSE IN A HURRY
WE HAVE
WHILE YOU WAIT
SERVICE
DISCOUNT

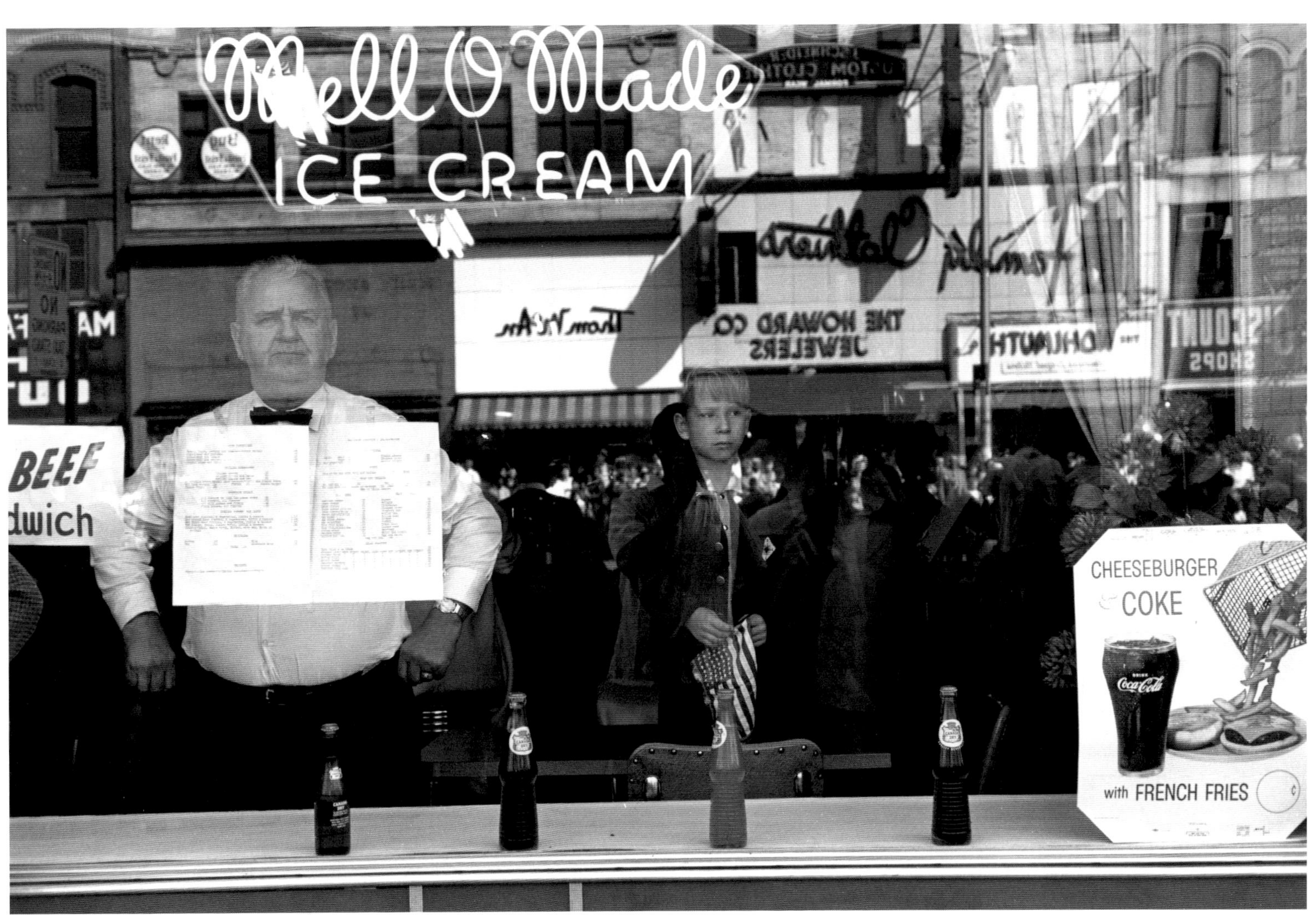
Mell O Made
ICE CREAM
CHEESEBURGER
& COKE
Coca-Cola
with FRENCH FRIES
BEEF
dwich
THE HOWARD CO
JEWELERS
DISCOUNT
SHOPS

Hit that jive, Jack!

Put it in your pocket till I get back.

Goin' downtown to see a man

And I ain't got time to shake your hand.

Hit That Jive Jack
WRITTEN BY JOHN ALSTON/CAMPBELL "SKEETS" TOLBERT
AS SUNG BY NAT KING COLE

1. Monsey, NY, 1963

2. New York City, 1960

3. Philadelphia, 1964

4. Texas, 1965

5. Colorado, 1967

6. Waddy, KY, 1966

7. New York City, 1964

8. Los Angeles, 1965

9. New York City, 1965

10. New York City, 1965

11. Washington, DC, 1966

12. New York City, 1964

13. Washington, DC, 1968

14. Florida, 1963

15. New York City, 1967

16. New York City, 1965

17. Buffalo, 1968

18. Upstate NY, 1968

19. New York City, 1963

20. Newark, NJ, 1962

21. Los Angeles, 1970

22. Washington, DC, 1965

23. Los Angeles, 1965

24. New Orleans, 1969

25. Atlantic City, 1962

26. Atlantic City, 1968

27. Minneapolis, 1966

28. New York City, 1967

29. Washington, DC, 1965

30. Washington, DC, 1968

31. Houston, 1970

32. Dallas, 1965

33. Washington, DC, 1962

34–48. Columbus Day, Newark, NJ, 1962

Publication made possible by Mary Jo and Ted P. Shen, B.A. 1966, Hon. 2001; Helen D. Buchanan; Jane P. Watkins, M.P.H. 1979; and the Samuel Freeman Charitable Trust.

First published in 2013 by the
Yale University Art Gallery
P.O. Box 208271
New Haven, CT 06520-8271
www.artgallery.yale.edu

and distributed by
Yale University Press
P.O. Box 209040
New Haven, CT 06520-9040
www.yalebooks.com/art

Designed and typeset by Katy Homans
Separations by Thomas Palmer
Set in Gotham types
Printed at Meridian Printing, East Greenwich, RI, under the supervision of Danny Frank

ISBN 978-0-300-19108-0
Library of Congress Control Number: 2013930294

10 9 8 7 6 5 4 3 2 1

Cover illustrations: (front) detail of pl. 1; (back) pl. 48
Frontispiece: detail of pl. 26